Triumph Over Tragedy

A Story of
Forgiveness and Healing
by the daughter of
James Byrd Jr.

Jamie Byrd-Grant

Triumph Over Tragedy
Copyright © 2021 Jamie Byrd-Grant
All Rights Reserved

This book or any portion thereof may not be reproduced or used in any manner whatsoever without the express written permission of the publisher except in the case of reprints in the context of reviews, quotes, or references. Although the publisher and the author have made every effort to ensure that the information in this book was correct at press time and while this publication is designed to provide accurate information in regard to the subject matter covered, the publisher and the author assume no responsibility for errors, inaccuracies, omissions, or any other inconsistencies herein and hereby disclaim any liability to any party for any loss, damage, or disruption caused by errors or omissions, whether such errors or omissions result from negligence, accident, or any other cause.

Printed in the United States of America
ISBN: 978-1-953497-21-5 (Print)
ISBN: 978-1-953497-22-2 (Digital)

Library of Congress Control Number: 2021914016

Published by Cocoon to Wings Publishing
7810 Gall Blvd. #311
Zephyrhills, FL 33541
www.CocoontoWingsBooks.com
(833) 343-7873 ext. 3

Scriptures marked NLT are taken from the HOLY BIBLE NEW LIVING TRANSLATION (NLT): Scriptures taken from the HOLY BIBLE, NEW LIVING TRANSLATION, Copyright ©1996, 2000, 2002, 2003 by Holman Bible Publishers, Nashville Tennesee. All rights reserved.

Scriptures marked NIV are taken from the NEW INTERNATIONAL VERSION (NIV): Scripture taken from THE HOLY BIBLE, NEW INTERNATIONAL VERSION® Copyright ©1973, 1978, 1984, 2011 by Biblica, Inc.™ Used by permission of Zondervan

Scriptures marked KJV are taken from the KING JAMES VERSION (KJV): KING JAMES VERSION, public domain.

All Scripture quotations are from The Passion Translation®. Copyright © 2017, 2018 by Passion & Fire Ministries, Inc. Used by permission. All rights reserved. ThePassionTranslation.com.

**News articles and associated images referenced in this book were reproduced with written permission from © BBC News from their coverage of the murder of James Byrd Jr. in the article titled, "Race in America: The legacy of the murder of James Byrd Jr."

Cover design by ETP Creative

Triumph Over Tragedy

Jamie Byrd-Grant

Contents

Acknowledgments 9

Dedication 11

Introduction 15

Letter to My Daddy 17

The Byrd Family 21

June 7, 1998 27

Once the Casket is Lowered 43

Is Normal Even Possible? 51

Grief and Greed 65

The Process of Forgiving While Remembering 77

It's A Movement Not A Moment 87

Finding Peace Within the Pain 101

Missing You 105

Reference 110

Memories 111

Acknowledgments

To my friend, soulmate, and husband, Sheldon Grant, thank you for encouraging and supporting me through this journey. To my son, Karter O'Rourke, who is my pride and joy, thank you for being my shining light at the end of the tunnel. To my "Hittas" - my sister, Renee Byrd Mullins, and brother, Ross Byrd, I couldn't ask for better siblings to walk this life's journey with. Thank you both for sharing some of the most unforgettable moments with Daddy that were a blur to me. As we often say, "We all we got!"

To Stephanie Outten and her team at Cocoon to Wings Publishing, thank you for helping me birth this book. Ereka Thomas' vision for the cover blew me away and brought me to tears. E. Claudette Freeman's editing skills helped me tell this story in the way you get to experience it. Everyone else on the team that I did not interact with personally, my heartfelt thanks go out to you.

Dedication

This book is in memory of my father, James Byrd Jr.

To The Most High, my Heavenly Father, thank you for choosing me to be a vessel of strength for others.

This book is also dedicated to my mother, Thelma Adams, for instilling in me the importance of forgiveness. Thank you for being my confidante, my friend, my rock, and, most of all, a loving and caring mother.

Dear Momma,

There are not enough words to express how much I adore and appreciate you; that's why I strive to show you daily. Although you are small and petite in stature, you carry the heart of a giant. You were just 20 years old, expecting your first child, when "Maw-Maw" gained her heavenly wings. I know losing your mother changed your life forever. You had to undergo so many challenges and life experiences without your mother's guidance. I can't imagine having to go through that. I will forever cherish the time you spent with me after I gave birth to Karter. From labor to delivery, to five months after Karter's arrival, to the weekly FaceTime sessions, to the weekend visits, you were there every step of the way. For as long as I can remember, I've prayed that God would grant me the opportunity for my kids to not only meet my parents, but to have a long-lasting relationship with them. All I can say is, through it all, "I am grateful." I'm grateful my son has the chance to have you in his life. I am indebted to you for the sacrifices you have made for our family. Without a doubt, you have always put your family's needs before your own. You make motherhood look easy.

Momma, I never told you this, but I admire your bravery for going to Huff Creek that Sunday night after the dragging death of Daddy. Grandpa thought it was absurd and tried to talk you out of witnessing such a petrifying scene. But there was no stopping you. You wanted to make sure that the investigation and identifying information were factual, that it was really Daddy. That's the type of heart you have! It was hard to believe, due to Daddy being well-known, that anyone would commit such a heinous and gruesome crime against him. Not that you had anything to prove, but that certainly validated your love for him by going there. You suppressed your pain that night when you unselfishly walked the streets of a community that you grew up in as a child. I remember you later told me that you "just had to see it for yourself." You wanted to know first-hand what happened to the man who was once the love of your life and father of your three kids. Little did you realize that night would later answer questions that no one else would have been able to answer for your children, and for me, it brought some closure.

    I thank you for teaching me to know God and to call on Him at all times, and not just in sorrow. Without God being the center of my life and your motherly guidance, I don't know where I would be. At times, when I feel like giving up, I think about you as a young mother sitting at the bus stop one night, when three thugs drove up in a pick-up truck and pointed a rifle to your head demanding you to get in the truck. Your life flashing before your eyes. Glory to God for sending His angels to protect you. Things certainly haven't been a cake walk, but you never gave up on life and what God had in store for you.

    Momma, I thank you from the bottom of my heart for being who you are. You are the most God-fearing, caring, loving, compassionate, and genuine person I have ever known. I am honored and forever grateful to call you my mother.

Love you forever and a day,

Your Baby, Jamie

Introduction

Triumph Over Tragedy is a short, but detailed account of the life and death of James Byrd Jr., the 49-year-old black man who was brutally murdered by three white supremacists in Jasper, Texas. On June 7, 1998, Byrd was savagely beaten, his face sprayed with black paint, and he was tied to the back of a pick-up truck and dragged for over three miles down a rural road in deep East Texas. His tall thin body was decapitated and dismembered. Parts of his body were discarded throughout the predominantly African American community of Huff Creek.

Imagine waking up and walking onto your front porch to the unsettling sight of a human head or leg lying in your yard, or even visiting your loved one's gravesite and stumbling upon freshly placed human remains. His death reawakened the many years of racism and hatred of black people in the small East Texas town. This horrific murder forced the passage of The James Byrd Jr. State Hate Crimes Act and a Federal Hate Crimes Act - James Byrd Jr. and Matthew Shepard Hate Crimes Prevention Act.

After many years of hatred, unforgiveness, and rage, as the daughter of a hate crime victim and a victim of that crime myself, I am sharing my struggles of overcoming hate and how I channel my energy to forgive, while never forgetting the dragging death of my father - a heinous murder that shook the world. This book explores my life experiences from the mind of a sixteen-year-old through adulthood. I go into the dark place of missing my dad, especially when he could no longer fulfill my number one dream of walking me down the aisle. When my dream became my worst nightmare and my nightmare became an unfathomable reality, what did I do? Where did I turn for help to process the incomprehensible? Join me as I embark on my journey of healing and restoration.

Letter to My Daddy

Hey Daddy,

Sitting here lounging on my chaise, thinking about all the things that have taken place over the last 23 years since you've been gone. AND BOY, has it been A LOT! Daddy, I hope you know how much I miss and love you! There aren't many days that go by without me thinking of you. Life's just not the same without you and so much has happened that I wish you were here to experience with me. It has been on my heart to start this new journey and now that I've finally taken that leap, I wanted to share some things with you that are long overdue.

I remember June 6, 1998. Me, Momma, and Renee were in the driveway of Grandma's house getting ready to head back to Lufkin and you didn't want us to leave. We sat in the car for well over an hour, going back and forth with you, until Aunt Mylinda convinced you to let us get on the road before night fall. Yea, the day your baby girl was being flip at the mouth all because I wanted to hurry back to Lufkin to hang out with friends, but you wanted to spend more time with us. Having all this time to think about it, hanging out with friends should never have been more important than spending time with you. I had NEVER disrespected you in any way, and that day, in the car, when I told you I hated you, shouldn't have been any different. But it was. And I did. To this day, it is one of the most regrettable moments of my life. Not realizing how hurtful those three words were until they were released from my lips. That moment has stuck with me in the worst way. For many years I felt guilty for your death. I blamed myself in so many ways, saying, "it wouldn't have happened if we had stayed in Jasper. If we visited your new apartment." You were so proud of having something to call your own, and I dimmed your light. You just wanted the women in your life to be proud of you and your accomplishments. I dishonored that by choosing my friends over you. Afterall, this was the moment we all had prayed for, and I allowed my selfish, self-centered actions to ruin the joys that had come true for you.

Daddy, I apologize for telling you "I HATE YOU" as we sat, talking in the car. All you wanted was to spend more time with your family. I could tell by the look on your face that you were not only in disbelief, but shocked and terribly disappointed with my lack of respect for you. My prayer has always been that those hurtful words from the 16-year-old me who was acting spoiled, selfish, and inconsiderate at the time, did not linger in your heart.. They came from a 16-year-old who was acting selfish and inconsiderate. Over the years, I've battled with forgiving myself because, little did I know, those three words would be our last. For many years, I secretly carried a great deal of shame, embarrassment, and anger. Because I had a habit of having a smart mouth, I remember Mama and Renee overlooking my comment that day as if it never happened, but that mouthy moment left a deep stain in my heart; wishing it were all a dream and that I would soon awaken to your witty personality and loud singing.

Those shameful words kept me in bondage. I've not been able to be the best version of myself at times. I remember reading Acts 3:19 where it says, "Repent then, and turn to God, so that your sins may be wiped out, that times of refreshing may come from the Lord." Daddy, I need a renewed and fresh start. Now that I've repented for my sinful ways, Daddy, I ask that you please forgive me. Forgive me for being disrespectful. I hope you knew those words were not of my character nor from my heart. They were unprocessed words with no meaning intended. I often wonder if things would have been different if we had gone to your apartment. "Only if" was a constant thought of mine. After years of wondering if you ever forgave me, I started having feelings of self-blame, feelings of guilt, self-shame, and disappointment. I had to pull myself together and ask God to forgive that sixteen-year-old because, while internalizing so many mixed emotions, I became shielded in accepting what God was trying to reveal to me.

As I'm writing this letter to you, I feel the spirit of God telling me you forgave me a long time ago. You forgave me in that very moment. Daddy, I thank you for looking past my immaturity and selfish ways. My heart is overjoyed knowing that you were just waiting on me to forgive myself.

Daddy, I can't wait to share some of my life experiences with you, such as becoming a mother. Yea, your baby girl has a baby boy and is happily married to the love of my life. I'm sure you were wondering what took me so long! HAAAHAA! Until next time, Daddy!

Love,

Your Baby girl!

The Byrd Family

My paternal family was always close-knit and unique. There's a bunch of Byrds, and we love food and sitting around telling old stories. Music has always been the heart of our family. Everyone likes to sing, but my dad was the total package. He could sing, play musical instruments, and he was the jokester of the family. Everyone gravitated toward him as the "clown of the family." In my heart, he was my grandparents' favorite of their eight children.

My grandparents, James Byrd Sr. and Stella Mae, were loving and very nurturing. They made sure that whenever my dad didn't do for us, they took up the slack for him. They picked us up in the summer, bought us school clothes so we wouldn't miss out on anything. They did extra for me and my siblings; and they favored us.

My grandmother was funny. The Byrd family is known to be full-figured, so she would always try to feed me. "Gal, when you gonna gain weight," she would ask. When I did begin to gain weight, she would say, "Gal, you look NICE." At my grandparent's home, by 10a.m. dinner was cooked, and breakfast was on the table. Nine o'clock at night, lights were out. At Vacation Bible School, she wanted us to shine. We had to be the ones to say the Bible verses and sing in the choir. We had to be in the front so she could proudly say, "Those James' kids."

Grandpa was a man of few words. Gentle. Quiet. Sat on the porch. Most of what he asked was, "How's school?" while his cigar hung from his lips. He talked to my brother, Ross, more than he did with me. Treated me like a baby. He walked around chewing on his unlit cigar all his life, wearing his suspenders attached to his dark brown pants and a white t-shirt. That was his daily look.

My dad has one brother and six sisters. James Byrd Jr. was the second oldest of the siblings. They grew up close and bonded over cooking. My family ate that "greasy meat," (a lot of fatty selections) but made sure we had quality vegetables picked from my grandmother's backyard. When we had family reunions, everybody would bring whatever and we had an over-abundance of food. Nothing was ever coordinated, but it always came together flawlessly. Seeing the smile on my grandparents' face when my aunts took over in the kitchen was a joy. We didn't vacation or travel as a family, but we spent a lot of time together in my younger days.

We have a ton of cousins. There are over twenty grandkids on the Byrd side. On my mom's side, the Adams Family, there is also a bunch of us. She has eight siblings, and they all grew up in Huff Creek in Jasper, Texas. My dad was considered a city-boy because he lived "up-town," while my mom was considered a country girl.

Her family grew up in the church. The creek was their swimming pool. That was the most excitement they had. My maternal grandmother, Francis, led the choir so they spent many days at church. She had to raise three of her grandchildren because one of her daughters died from being poisoned in her 20s by a woman who was jealous of her for dating a particular man. Grandma Francis died at the age of 56, and to this day, my mom says her sister's death took its toll on her.

Grandpa Oscar (mom's dad) was just like my other grandfather. Quiet. When he did talk, he had a little rasp in his voice. I was a young child visiting my grandpa in a nursing home. He had one leg amputated. I knew I was his favorite. He would say to my mom, "Where's that little girl?" I would sit in the bed with him and chew his food up to feed it to him. He loved burgers and fries, that's probably where my adoration of them came from, and I love fries to this day. My family would call me "potato chip" because I would eat anything related to chips and fries.

My parents, Thelma and James, met at J.H. Rowe High School, which was segregated. He was a proud graduate of the Class of 1967 and she in 1968. He liked her, but my mom was a tomboy. She says her mind was not on dating, so she didn't take him seriously until - one night. Everyone recognized how talented and gifted my dad was, especially musically. He was known as "Purple Rain," an ode to music artist Prince, because of his stellar singing ability. Imagine how that stroked his ego. He was the main attraction at the Friday night football games, standing front and center, leading the band as he played the trumpet. My mom would share the stories of how he was the star of the night. The night he played "Wonderland by Night" by Bert Kaempfert was unforgettable to many Jasper natives, especially my mother. That did it for her! That was one moment in time she said she'll never forget, the night she fell in "inexpressible love" with him, as she likes to say. From that day forward they started to date, and three years later, they tied the knot. Becoming a 20-year-old newlywed and soon-to-be mother to my oldest sibling, Renee, was a big adjustment for my mom. My mother shared that the joy my sister brought to her was unimaginable because she helped fill the pain of my maternal grandmother's death. It's amazing how God will replace pain with joy.

My mother told us that during their honeymoon phase my dad would often sing to her. If he didn't know the words you would never notice because he would sing the melody so well and on tune, giving you the impression that he wrote the song. I often wondered what song he would have sung to me during our daddy-daughter dance at my wedding. The melody to "Dance with My Father," by Luther Vandross plays in my head whenever I think about it.

When my sister was 6 years old, my parents got pregnant again but the baby, which they named Rolando, was stillborn. Three years later, they were blessed with the birth of my brother, Ross and then I came three years after that. My parents were married for about seventeen years before things got rocky, and six years later they got divorced. Even though they were divorced, they maintained a good relationship, which is why he would show up unexpectedly. From what I saw, neither of them ever moved on to any other real relationships. My siblings and I were resolved with them not being together because it didn't impact how they raised us as parents.

Over the course of five years, after my parents divorced, Ross graduated from high school, went to college to play football, and then enlisted in the military. Renee also went to the military after graduation but was honorably discharged in 1996 due to a disability. I was in high school then, hanging out at the mall and with friends at their houses, but I always enjoyed times with my family in Jasper.

Reflections

- What is your favorite family memory that you still hold onto?

_____
_____
_____
_____
_____
_____
_____
_____
_____

- What was your favorite family vacation or gathering? What were some of the things that made this occasion special?

June 7, 1998

June 6, 1998 - A Bridal Shower

One June 6, 1998, my mom, sister, and I were running around town trying to find the perfect gift for my cousin's bridal shower. We were running around in a panic as if the shower wasn't on our calendars for a month of Sundays. We were notorious procrastinators. My mom would always say, "Don't sweat the small stuff, it will be fine."

After three hours of shopping, we settled on buying nightgowns for the bride-to-be. I couldn't leave the mall without buying the perfect outfit for me--a dress that was half-denim, half floral, and hit right above my knees. My mom dreaded going shopping with me, as if I needed more junk, she would often say. My mom would sit on the mall benches while I tried on every single piece to make sure it all fit. I had my own creative fashion sense and wanted everything to be perfect. After making my final selections, we proceeded to the cashier. My mom whipped out her Bealls card to pay for the items, and we were excitedly on our way home to get dressed and head out of town. I was more excited because, in my family, small gatherings such as baby showers, bridal showers, and even kids' birthday parties, always turned into a family reunion. I couldn't wait to see all my cousins who would be traveling from "H-Town." (H-Town is what millennials called Houston, Texas). Jasper, Texas was about fifty-eight miles from Lufkin, Texas where we lived. My mom was the most law-abiding driver; she would go the exact speed limit, which always put us right at an hour drive to Jasper instead of the normal forty-five minutes for most people. Let's just say when my uncles were driving, it would be more like a thirty to forty-minute drive. My mom used to call them "Speedy Gonzales," a term from an old cartoon about the fastest mouse in Mexico and his adventures. I would turn on my mom's favorite tunes hoping the beats would encourage her to accelerate a little bit. "Ice, Ice Baby," by Vanilla Ice, was her all-time favorite jam, but it didn't work. Her jamming to the music didn't increase the force on the accelerator. We coasted along at 50 miles an hour. She would jokingly say, "Why we rushing, flushing." I just didn't want to miss out on anything. I wanted to be present for it all.

The minute we hit the family home in Jasper, I hooked up with my three closest cousins and the girl chat began. We would go for hours exchanging stories. When I would spend the night, we would sometimes talk into the wee hours. My aunt Betty would periodically get up throughout the night and tell us to cut the lights off and go to bed. No matter what was going on, Aunt Betty was in the bed by 6 p.m. and couldn't for the life of her understand why we kept late night hours. She would wake up by 3 a.m. and start cleaning, cooking, and would even make a trip to Wal-Mart. She would have her day completed before everyone else woke up.

My cousins and I chatted about boys, school, and all the latest entertainment news. Being Houston residents, they knew more than I did about the hottest celebrity gossip. Being from Lufkin, I was never exposed to any of that. Running into Beyoncé was common for them, while going on trail rides and to the Houston Livestock Show and Rodeo was my normal. It appears there was always something to do in Houston. *I can't wait to live there* was my constant thought. But reality set in, and I had to remember we were in Jasper for my cousin's bridal shower where there was plenty of food and entertainment.

My brother, Ross, was in Basic Training in the Army, so he couldn't be with us that time. After the bridal shower, everyone gathered at my grandparents' house. The kids ran around outside while the grown-ups laughed at each other's tall tales and played cards and dominos. Shortly after we got there, the "life of the party" arrived – my dad. You couldn't pay my dad to attend the bridal shower, although there were other men present. He figured bridal and baby showers were strictly for females. As he walked into the house, he gave hugs and high-fives as he passed my aunts and uncles. No matter where the kids were and what they were doing, when he arrived everyone gravitated towards him, knowing he was about to make everyone laugh.

In my grandparents' home, certain people had special seating, and he was one of those special people. He walked past Grandma, as she sat in her famous burgundy recliner, and sat in the recliner across from Grandpa. As he walked, it was like he was running away from something. He had a look on his face like he had to get to the seat quickly to sit down. As he was posturing to sit down, he released a sigh of relief. But he landed on a balloon in the chair left by one of my little cousins. The balloon popped, and all I could see was my dad grab his heart and jump up quickly. I heard someone say, "You thought someone shot you?" He had a worried look, and his mouth was wide open as if he tried to scream, but nothing came out. To this day, I'll never know if his worried look was because he was afraid or because he was embarrassed by all the attention. He never liked folks catering to him, so I chalked it up to embarrassment. He quickly gathered his composure and sat stiffly in the chair. While he would entertain anybody that would clap, and bring rounds of laughter, it didn't take long to notice he was bothered by the popping of the balloon. Everyone kept asking him, "Son, are you okay?" "Son" was my father's nickname because he was the first-born son to his parents. His reply, in a nonchalant, calm manner was, "Why wouldn't I be?" Everything went back to normal, and we sat around talking about the bridal shower. I went to sit on the armrest of the recliner next to my dad. We chitchatted a bit about school, even though it was summer, and school was out. That was his way of starting conversations with me, no matter what time of year.

A Fight

After visiting with my dad, we decided to head back home to Lufkin. Everyone was packing up to head home, some family members were traveling as far as Louisiana, Houston, and

Beaumont. Dad hurried and jumped in the back seat with me when he noticed we were also headed out. He kept trying to convince us to stay at his place for the night. He offered to make us steak and potatoes at his new place. He was extremely proud of his new apartment because he had been living with his parents for about a year, and the apartment represented him being back on his feet, starting fresh again. Even though he was 49 years old, Grandma still had rules to her house. He couldn't come and go as he pleased, and he better not come in the house past 10 o'clock or the latch would be on the door. I'm sure that's why he was so excited to be in his own place. He was not a cook, so the steak and potatoes were clearly a way of bribing us to stay.

Mom and Dad had been long divorced but were great friends. I knew my dad still had the hots for Mom, but he was too shy to say it. To this day, my mom says he always had a funny way of showing his true feelings and affection. To picture such an outgoing, worldly guy being shy is something to witness. He was never very affectionate. He wouldn't just grab my mom and say, "I love you." He spoke around his words and would say, "Girl, you know I love you!" He was very guarded. Instead of giving his girls hugs, he would pat us on the head or play with our hair as a sign of his affection.

After repeatedly asking us to go to his place, I grew irritated. I had plans to hang out with friends, so we needed to hurry back to Lufkin. I remember saying to myself, *He picked a fine time to invite us over.* Any other time I would have loved to visit and wouldn't have wanted to leave his place, but all I could think about was the house party that had long been on my to-do list. My aunt even tried asking him to let us get on the road before it got dark, but he kept insisting on "grilling steaks for my family." He was so proud in announcing his plans. As the hours and night fall grew closer, all I could think of was that my friends were out having fun without me. I turned to my dad and said, "Please let us go."

He told me to stay in a child's place and to watch my tone when talking to him. "You don't call no shots, little girl!" That's what he said. I, without thought, screamed, "WE HAVE TO GO! I HAVE THINGS TO DO!" We exchanged heated words; then, finally my mom yelled at me from the driver's seat to calm down and stop talking back because my days would be shortened. I turned to my dad and yelled, "I HATE YOU!"

Everything stopped and everyone in the car turned to me with shock covering their faces. I could hear the air blowing from the vents of the car and everything seemed to be going in slow motion. I replayed those harsh words in my mind. I wanted to take those words back, but it all seemed unreal then. Dad's long wide fingers reached for the door handle, opening the door as slowly as he could. All he uttered was, "Y'all be safe on the road." At the sound of the door shutting, I came back to myself. *What just happened?* I talked myself out of going anywhere. That was the longest hour ride back to Lufkin in all the years we'd made the drive. The quietness from my mom and sister made me feel how disappointed they were in my poor choice of words. My mom would often say, "If you keep your mouth closed, people won't know how ignorant you are." That moment without a doubt was my ignorant moment, and I regret it every day.

The next day was a typical sunny Sunday. Mom was cooking her gourmet breakfast as usual, while my sister, who had flown in from Hawaii for my maternal uncle's funeral and stayed for the bridal shower, was sitting at the kitchen table feeding her baby girl. I was cleaning up the living room, which was adjacent to the kitchen. We were reminiscing about the fun time we had the day before despite my selfish moment. Although my parents were divorced, my dad's side of the family didn't treat my mom any different. Matter of fact, Grandma never stopped claiming her as one of her daughters. We just couldn't get over how clingy my dad was that night. I mean, he was always glad to see us, but for a man that normally didn't cook, to offer us steak and potatoes was surprisingly shocking and cute at the same time.

A Call, Life Changes

We were still talking about my dad being clingy and laughing about how he was flirting with my mom. As laughter filled the room, the phone rang sounding like a fire alarm. My sister, still laughing as she answered the phone, noticed that it was one of my aunts. "HEY AUNTIE," she was seemingly excited as she answered. Her excitement instantly became silence, and then a loud thump on the wall echoed from the hallway. "NO, DADDY! NO, NO," rang from my sister's mouth. My mom and I ran into the hallway to find my sister on her knees screaming, "NOOOOO!" There I was wondering what my auntie could have possibly said to make such a giddy laugh turn into the most gut-wrenching cry. It wasn't until after my dad's homegoing that my sister told me what my aunt said on the phone that day. All my aunt kept saying was, "It's Son! It's really bad. Y'all get down here now." As she began to get up off the wood floor, my sister threw the white cordless phone on the brown sofa stating, "We have to get to Jasper." She never hung up the phone, so I could still hear my aunt on the phone saying, "YALL GET DOWN HERE. IT'S SON! GET DOWN HERE NOW." I stood there in a daze as my sister was hollering and crying. My mom came from the kitchen, looked at the phone for a second and could hear the dial tone after my aunt hung up.

Everything happened so quick from there. Momma hung up the phone, we all threw on some clothes and hopped in the car to drive to Jasper. My sister, Renee, drove. I don't even recall the hour-long drive to Jasper. We got there so quick; it was like one of my uncles was driving. As we arrived at my grandparents', the front of the house was surrounded by media vans and law enforcement. I'd never seen so many police cars in one spot in my life. As I approached the driveway, mounds of people came out of nowhere. People were pulling and hugging on us as we attempted to walk up the driveway of my grandparents' home. I felt as if I was in a deep sleep and people were calling my name trying to awaken me.

As I finally broke away from the masses of people swarming around me, like bees to a beehive, I walked into my grandparents' living room which was standing-room-only. I could usually see my grandmother from the time I walked in the house from the position of her recliner, but there were so many people surrounding her, I had to peel through people to get to her. I remember squeezing by a tall, thin man and several sheriffs just to get to Grandma. I later found out the tall thin man was Rev.

Jessie Jackson. I remembered hearing his name growing up; my mom would always mention him, Rev. Dr. Martin Luther King, Jr., and several other activists. There he was, an icon, standing tall and upright, in my grandparents' home.

Although I had a feeling whatever happened was bad, I didn't want to know what had taken place. Not then. It was too much to take in. Too confusing. At that time. I dashed down the hall to the left and into my dad's old room, before he moved into his own place. My dad's scent filled the room as if he were present and never moved out. As I sat on the bed, my cousin entered asking me if I wanted to know what happened to Uncle Byrd. That's what my cousins called him. Still in denial, I asked, "What do you mean 'what happened' to my daddy? Nothing is wrong with him. I don't understand why all of these people are here." She decided not to push me, so we started to talk about general things to distract me from what was really happening. Missy and I had always clicked. Months could pass without our seeing each other, but once we were together, our conversations picked up right where we had left them. This time she was doing most of the talking and I was listening. As much as I tried to block out all the noise from the droves of people storming into my grandparents' home, I couldn't help but to listen as I acted engaged in Missy's conversation. My mind was telling me this wasn't good, that something bad had happened, but my heart didn't want to accept what my mind was telling me. During the entire conversation, I prayed that at any moment my dad would walk through the door of my grandparent's home.

As the days went by, different people stopped by to pray and to drop off food and cards. I sat on the swing set on the front porch, swinging, trying not to pay attention to the people. I looked up the steep hill near my grandparents' house and there he was – Daddy. My daddy. He was wearing dark denim jeans and a blue and white button-down shirt, which was unbuttoned. As he walked, the wind blew his shirt open showing off his small frame, yet masculine chest. I jumped off the swing screaming, "Daddy!" I ran toward him. Just like that, he was gone. The vision of him –gone. I stood at the end of the driveway reaching out to thin air. I still had hope. Whatever people were saying wasn't true. It had to be mistaken identity or something. They could not have killed my daddy. A week later, the day before my dad's homegoing celebration, my cousin asked me again if I wanted to know what happened to "Uncle Byrd." I pondered for a while before saying, "Yes, what happened?" Calmly, she told me everything she knew.

Uncle Byrd went to a friend's party. As he was walking home, three white men picked him up and they took him to Huff Creek where they tied him to a pickup truck and drug him to death.

I was in total denial. I didn't cry. Couldn't fathom what she was saying. Part of me knew it was true because of the funeral preparations being made. The other part of me felt it couldn't be true. I went to the restroom, sat on the toilet, replaying everything in my head. I envisioned him walking down the road. I envisioned every part of the story she told me. Tears came. I wiped them. I walked back into the room as if nothing happened. I couldn't show emotion. Didn't want to.

I later discovered that he was only a few blocks away from my grandparents' home when the men abducted him. He was savagely beaten, his face sprayed with black paint, and he was tied to the back of their pick-up truck where he was dragged to his death for over three miles down a rural road in deep East Texas. His tall thin body was decapitated and dismembered. Parts of his body were found throughout the predominately African American community of Huff Creek, a small residential area in the town of Jasper. Imagine waking up and walking out onto your front porch to the unsettling sight of a human head or leg lying in your yard or even visiting your loved one's gravesite and you stumble upon freshly placed human remains.

During the investigation, my family learned that there was an eyewitness that saw my dad in the truck and was able to describe it for investigators. There was another lead - a young black boy who stumbled upon my dad's remains early that Sunday morning as he was headed to church. Because he was young, I'm unclear on if he called the local Sheriff's Department, or if he told an adult who called. Either way, the local Sheriff's Department was called due to Huff Creek's size. Once the Sheriffs arrived, they realized Dad's killing required special attention, so they called in the FBI for backup on this investigation. It didn't take long for the news to spread throughout the small town. This was one of worst hate crimes America had seen.

I never thought something like this could happen in my lifetime or to my family. What family does? This was the most horrific crimes I'd ever heard of or read about. It was a horrible nightmare; and I wanted someone to awaken me before it got worse. We were told that there would be no viewing of the body. This didn't sit well with me. I needed to see if it was really my dad. I still had hope. Being a kid, I didn't fully grasp that his body was tortured as bad as they described; identifying him would be hard. His dentures and photo identification were found at one the scenes, which was the only way to identify him. The week after his murder and leading up the funeral I blocked out all noise.

I isolated myself in my pink and grey bedroom. I collected stuffed animals, which were all neatly placed on the side of the bed opposite of where I slept. They became my confidantes. When what truly happened to my dad hit me, I buried my head in my stuffed animals and screamed and cried. I fully and completely cried. I cried so hard it shocked me. I had never cried like that before, and I couldn't let my mom hear my pain. I didn't want to stress her out, she was already incredibly worried about me and my siblings, especially my brother because he was a Black boy.

My tears, then, weren't because of his killing, they were because of what happened between the two of us before he passed away. My guilt was all I could process at the time. The grief came later. There's nothing more heartbreaking to know, in the natural, I could never say, "I'm sorry." Questions began racing through my mind. *Why me? Did he forgive me? Did he suffer? How do I forgive myself?* June 7, 1998 was the worst day of my life.

REPRODUCED PORTIONS OF THE VIDEO ARTICLE, Race in America: The legacy of the murder of James Byrd Jr. FROM BBC NEWS[1]

Father Ron Foshage
"One of the worst hate crimes this nation has ever seen. Byrd was kidnapped, and then tied behind a pickup truck and dragged for nearly three miles in the East Texas city of Jasper all because he was Black."

Narrator
"The legacy of a gruesome hate crime still haunts this small Texas town."

Angel San Juan
"Their lives changed forever on June 7, the day of Byrd's murder."

Angel San Juan
"There are not words to describe just how bad this was."

Father Ron Foshage
"We learned that there was a great deal of prejudice in our community that we kind of swept under the rug."

Narrator
"And it changed one family forever."

Narrator
"On a Saturday night, in June 1998, James Byrd Jr. caught a ride with three white men in Jasper, Texas. They drove him down a dark country road, beat him, and then chained him alive to a pickup truck and dragged his body for three miles, until he was decapitated."

Father Ron Foshage
"A black boy found the body on his way to church, and he called the sheriff's department because it was outside of the city limits."

Narrator
"The sheriff immediately called the FBI in for backup. But it didn't take long for the news to spread through town."

Father Ron Foshage
"He took the ministers out there and showed us. And we saw where the teeth were and where the baseball cap was and where the arm and the head were. And it was horrible."

Reflections

- What do you do when your worst nightmare becomes an unfathomable reality?

- Where do you turn for help to process the incomprehensible?

___

> **Bible verse:** "But you Lord, do not be far from me. **You are my strength**, come quickly to help me" (Psalms 22:19 NIV).

Once the Casket is Lowered

Silenced Emotions

My dad's murder was an awakening for the town. Blacks and Whites were surprised by the magnitude of what happened. It wasn't uncommon for Black folks to come up missing in Jasper. But what happened to my dad was the most horrific thing to ever happen there. His murder brought the town together.

A swift investigation ensued. A lighter, with something related to the Aryan Brotherhood, had been left at the scene. It was discovered that the killers had gone through the car wash, and the car wash attendant provided the FBI with a lead on the type of truck. He described seeing blood and a chain hanging from the truck. When the FBI got to the apartment, they found the truck with the chain.

Inside their apartment, the FBI found damning materials about the three men, who had recently been released from prison. Investigators found a copy of The Turner Diaries, which is a white supremacist guide, along with a letter describing the plans for them to lynch a black man. They also mentioned starting a KKK group in Jasper. To start the group, they had to do something horrific to spark the attention of potential initiates. Killing my dad was their spark.

Through the investigation, DNA was taken from my dad's shoes, hat, and wallet, and the DNA matched that of the white supremacists. They were captured and arrested the day after killing my dad. To add insult to injury, we learned that the murderers celebrated killing my dad by going to a BBQ afterward. The head Sheriff in Jasper went to my grandmother's house to notify her. My mom, sister, and I were already back home in Lufkin when my Aunt Betty called. That was the phone call that changed our lives. The entire investigation and the arrests had already taken place by the time we received the phone call telling us to get to Jasper.

In the year between my father's murder and the trial, my siblings and I, along with my grandmother and aunts, did a lot of speaking engagements. My grandmother wanted peace amid the pain. The Black Panthers had come to Jasper to spark riots. Dollies with mounds of mail was coming in from schools across the country. Elementary school kids from across the world wrote letters specifically to me to encourage me and tell me there was no place for hate. Joan Kroc, the last wife of McDonald's founder, Ray Kroc, reached out wanting to be my godmother. She even sent a check to my grandmother for me.

While my family was speaking peace, I was very vocal about my hatred for the thugs who murdered my daddy. I recall being on the Mother Love "Forgive and Forget" show, and I spoke up saying that I wanted to see them tied up and drug behind a truck until death just like they killed my daddy.

As Mother Love continued to question, I just couldn't see it in my heart to forgive them for torturing my dad. I couldn't even envision the wildest animal being slain the way my dad was. How could I forgive someone for something so cruel and inhumane? During the segment breaks, several audience members homed in on me more than my sister. Perhaps they understood why I carried so much anger. Renee was always so soft spoken, and through her eyes you could see the compassion and love she had for all people. I battled with my feelings, not only were they quite different than my sister's but my mother's as well. Deep down inside I wanted to have that same pure heart of forgiveness, but I couldn't. I wanted people to feel my pain, my anger, and, most importantly, I wanted people to know that it was okay to be angry. It's what you do with the anger that becomes a sin. For me, I had constant thoughts of taking matters into my own hands if I ever saw the murderers. I would dream about them being dragged behind a pickup truck and being dismembered like my dad. But those were thoughts that I never allowed to manifest into something real.

My brother, Ross, was allowed to come home from Basic Training due to a "family emergency." He was told by his Sergeant that he had an important phone call he had to take. Hearing him talk about it in more recent years, he said, "I tell you, that's one phone call that you don't ever want to get."

He was home with us for about a month before he had to go back. Initially, when he was in Basic Training, he did not have a roommate. Ross had pictures of me, my mom, and sister on his television stand in his barracks. When he did go back to training, they had moved a roommate in with him. Ross discovered that the pictures of us were turned face down and a confederate flag was hanging on the wall over his new white roommate's bed. The shock of seeing this caused Ross to rail on him and beat him badly. Ross called my mom to come get him. My mom and I drove to Louisiana to pick him up. He was honorably discharged with full benefits. To this day, he says he left the military because he couldn't fathom "fighting for a country that killed his old man."

By the time the first murder trial came, in Jasper, in 1999, I was over all of it. I was tired of all the speaking engagements, media, everything! --While attending the first trial, my brother, grandfather, and I decided to excuse ourselves. Rage erupted in my stomach because of the things I was hearing. We were warned before the trial that aggressive actions or outbursts could jeopardize the case. That felt like a slap in the face to censor a family who understandably should have been outraged. I didn't want to be the one whose rage exploded into loud and angry words, so I knew I needed to get out of there. I stood, but my first step felt as if I was trying to walk through quicksand. I could no longer feel my feet. Thankfully, my brother was there to guide me out of the courtroom. The exit doors seemed to drift further and further away. On the other side of the doors, the media swarmed us as we attempted our great escape. When we finally made it outside, I felt a gust of hot air hit me in the face as if we were in the middle of a hurricane. I didn't care. I just wanted OUT! Taking the first steps onto pavement, my legs weakened, and I fell into the arms of my big brother. My uncontrollable – though justifiable - emotions would not be a reason for the case to be thrown out. They didn't have to worry about me. While some members of my family continued to attend the trials, I decided to no longer attend.

The second trial was in Bryan, Texas. It was all over the news that Ku Klux Klan (KKK) rallies were happening all throughout the trial. My mom attended that trial and was infuriated that the KKK was there. By the time of the third trial, which was in Jasper, tension in the town was provoked between the Nation of Islam and the Ku Klux Klan when the Nation of Islam tried to pass through a police barricade. Members of the Klan posted in the streets with their flags displaying pride in the evil and inhumane murder of my dad. The Nation of Islam was reportedly there in protest of dad's murder, to present a united show of solidarity and – some even said – to protect our family and other Black residents of Jasper.

Some would say Jasper is a small, family-oriented town displaying no racial division. Others would strongly state otherwise. This region's past also comes into play because this part of Texas had a long history of slavery and racial violence in the aftermath of Reconstruction. It was not surprising for a black man to be reported missing mysteriously in Jasper and the surrounding areas, especially in the 1940s-1960s. Lynching was as prevalent in Texas as in the worst parts of the Deep South. After the dragging death of my dad, there was another black male, a native of Jasper, found dead outside of the city limits. Rumors say a white police officer was involved in his murder, but that was never confirmed. His body was found by family and friends who had been searching for him during the chilly winter months. Jasper and surrounding areas still operate off the good ole boy code. Public lynching of Black people became a common place in the East Texas towns. Someone saw and heard something, but no one felt obligated to say anything. This happens way too often when people fail to report a crime because it doesn't directly affect them.

A deadly situation that changed the trajectory of American history became a constant reminder for my family, even during the holidays. Driving from Lufkin to Jasper was a straight shot down Highway 63; those road trips were like no other. We used to have so much fun. The drive ceased being fun though. Our Thanksgiving and Christmas holidays were no longer the same. All the excitement was sucked out of our family gatherings. When we did gather, it was no longer at my grandparents' house. There was no more "Byrd Family" Day, no more family fishing, no more Vacation Bible School in the summer at my grandmother's house. Any time we went back to Jasper, after my father's murder, visits centered around dad's death. My family didn't have anything else to talk about anymore.

Grandma's house no longer smelled like pies, cakes, and good ole purple hull peas simmering. Our visits went from hearing my dad playing the piano while my grandparents stood over him singing their favorite church hymns, to my grandmother telling us about someone destroying his gravesite. Two white teenagers took pride in vandalizing the grave of a black man; that black man's grave happened to be James Byrd Jr's. They bragged about what they'd done to friends. But it didn't stop there. They found more fun and joy in pushing over the tombstones of others. This forced the family to surround his grave with an iron fence as a message to stop the vandalism. The teens were charged with criminal mischief, but there's always a copy-cat. Making a mockery out of desecrating his grave was hateful and disrespectful to my family. Evil should not have visited him at his resting place. Hadn't he gone through enough?

    I had constant anxiety after his gravesite was disturbed. It happened twice. I was scared to go back there because I was afraid of what I might see. Driving to Jasper became traumatizing for me. Seeing the Jasper city limits sign would unnerve me. Even driving through certain roads, rural areas would spark visions of Huff Creek and what happened to my dad. I could no longer go to Huff Creek, where my mom was raised. It took 18 years before I could muster up the courage to visit for the Huff Creek Church Homecoming, which happened every September in that community. I understood the fear that must have gripped my grandmother and my aunts, too, after that summer day. One of the things that highlights that fear to me about my Aunt Betty – though she never said it - was she no longer took those early morning drives to Walmart in preparation for her family again. I would wake up in the middle of the night in distress.

    While lying in bed, I would see my dad standing at the end of my bed. I knew he was watching over me. When I would fully wake up, the vision of him would vanish. Nightmares invaded my sleep. I could see myself running the murderers over with a car. See them in pieces across the street in that moment would satisfy me. *Daddy, I got them back* was temporary satisfaction for me. At a certain time of the night, I'm taken back to the night of my dad's murder. I can't explain it, but there's a certain way the sky will look that brings back the memory. It's as if I am being reminded of the time of night my dad was killed.

Reflections

- Have you ever experienced a time where your feelings were silenced?

_____

_____

- What was the situation, and why did you feel like you couldn't share your feelings?

_____

_____

_____

_____

_____

_____

Is Normal Even Possible?

But life had to continue. My high school years went by quickly, as I unimaginably had to grow up beyond my years.

Growing up with older siblings who were well known in school and around the neighborhood, was an automatic induction into the popular crowd for me. Being the daughter of James Byrd Jr. who was viciously killed also heightened my popularity. I have always been a very private person; some would say I was more of an introvert. Without seeking the attention that stemmed from our family's tragedy, it was coming from different directions. I had to think as a young adult with heavier responsibilities and not like a regular 16-year-old getting ready for prom.

I felt as if I was targeted during my later high school years; like people were waiting to see if my loving and outgoing character would change. I became extremely paranoid after one incident that reminded me my popularity wasn't necessarily a good thing. Three white boys attempted to run into my car as I was exiting the parking lot after school. It almost felt like a Lifetime Network movie. I thought, *this can't be happening to me.* I decided that I wouldn't be defeated by fear or hatred, so I continued to drive slowly towards the exit making little eye contact with them. Then, there we were, both cars sitting at the narrow exit waiting to see who was going to give up, one of the boys threw a soda can at my car. Yea, he was mad. I assumed my small Ford Escort intimidated or offended his big Dodge truck with a confederate flag on the back window. From that day forward my parking lot anxiety increased. I feared the unknown.

I kept myself active and involved with chores, school happenings, and extracurricular activities to keep my mind settled, if that was such a thing. I moved so fast all the time to avoid thinking about what happened. I figured if I stayed busy, everything would just go away. At that age, I didn't think about the fact that every year I would see the reminders of his murder. I was hoping that time would ease the pain of it. After the death of my dad, I became even more isolated. Being private and experiencing a lack of trust was not a good combination for a teenager. Childhood friends turned their back on me because I was no longer hanging out and going to parties. I stopped getting invited to things. I felt like I had a different mindset than the friends I was hanging out with. I was more focused on my safety. I was afraid to go out at night. After what happened to my father, I didn't want to be out late for fear that something could happen to me. It wasn't about them. It was my fears. I guess that was more than they could understand or care about. Other friends turned their back on me due to jealously, thinking that I was getting some glorified attention. Little did they know, I'd rather not have had any of it – not for the reason that it was being given.

Family that I'd never heard of suddenly started coming around. There were some things that showed up in other family members that I never expected. A family that was thicker than thieves became distant, and, in many ways, the enemy at times. After such a tragic situation and multiple trials, you would think everybody on both sides of my family would come together and be supportive, but I saw the opposite. What I thought were previously genuine relationships were no longer real. Everybody appeared to have a motive, and that motive was not in the best interest of Jamie. Walking around with a guarded heart was the worst thing I could've done. I just didn't know who to turn to, so I kept it all balled up inside.

Then there were local community activists who were taking advantage of my family by positioning themselves as the family representative. They befriended my grandparents so they could take advantage of them and be in the limelight. They would do interviews on behalf of the family, get pictures painted of my dad to auction them off. The money wasn't coming to us, or the foundation established in dad's honor. Some family members were chasing that same kind of clout. When financial resources or certain media opportunities were presented, they were there. My siblings and I have never gotten an apology from any of them. I still wonder if they understand the hurt and pain, they caused us by not allowing

Renee, Ross, and I to be included in EVERYTHING pertaining to our dad. The dust has since settled, and everything is back to some sense of normalcy in my family. *Will things ever be the way they used to be?* That's a question I still ask myself.

I began to shut down mentally and emotionally. Somehow, my body was still moving right along. I never spoke of dad's murder or the trials, not even to my closest friends. How could they understand? It wasn't a regular topic with us, and I preferred it that way. This was my way of staying strong, not knowing I was on a road to self-destruction. There weren't many family discussions. It seemed as if we avoided the conversation as well as listening to the local news. Whatever it took to escape the pain, even if that meant walking around in silence. This was incredibly challenging for my family because we had always been so open and comforting towards one another. Every family member was so deeply affected that our emotions wouldn't allow us to comfort one another.

I was nominated to be on the high school homecoming court three years in a row. The first year, my maternal uncle, Leroy, walked me up the field. The last two years, my brother had the honor. They each had to fill my Daddy-sized void by escorting me on the football field. I felt incomplete because it seemed I was the only one whose brother was escorting her. I was robbed of the full experience and joy of being nominated. I was consumed with the fact that I didn't have my daddy to walk with me. I felt out of place. My buddy, my brother was walking me up the field, while I watched the excitement on the other fathers' faces. They looked proud of their daughters, and while my brother and uncle were proud of me, it wasn't the same as having my dad with me. My maternal uncle was like a fill-in father, and since he was older, he fit in with the other fathers. While I love and appreciate my brother and uncle for who they are and what they did for me, they still weren't my dad. This was yet **another** emotional moment that left me with little to no time to worry about my emotions, so I silenced them and kept pushing, saying to myself, "I will deal with it when I'm alone." My alone didn't come until years later when I was in college and finally processed my hurt, pain, and feelings. Then, in reflective hindsight, I accepted my dad not being there for homecoming. Instead of being sad about the memories of those amazing nights (that I wanted to end quickly), I decided to appreciate the fact that I was nominated, and family was there for me. This was just the beginning of many fulfilled voids -- fulfilled because of my brother and uncle, yet unfulfilled because my Daddy wasn't there to do it with me as I strived to be successful and accomplished.

While all this "after the murder, trying to live normally again" was happening, I met someone. One day, my mom's friend had her son, Sheldon, drop her off at my mom's house. I answered the door. When I did, he signaled for me to come to the car. I walked to the car, and we started talking. We exchanged numbers. I was 17. He was 20 and in college. When he would drive back from college, I would meet him at the Jack in the Box restaurant in Lufkin. After about three meetings, he discovered I was too young for him, and he told me I "wasn't on his level." We lost touch and I started dating someone else. About a year later, I stood in the center of my grandparents' living room as I and two of my cousins were presented with full scholarships to Texas Southern University in memory of my dad. Although my heart was set on Louisiana State University, I was grateful for the full ride. There was nothing more exciting to look forward to.

Reflections:

- Were you ever able to go back to a "normal life" after tragedy knocked on your door?

_____

_____

- If so, what steps did you take to regain a sense of normalcy?

_____

_____

_____

_____

_____

_____

_____

So Many Questions...

When my dad was gruesomely slain, a piece of me was stolen. Denial, confusion, heartbreak, hurt, numbness, and outrage were always close at hand, and either emotion would hit me unexpectedly. Sometimes they were interchangeable, and other times they came as a package. What was I to do? How was I to feel? Where do I go from here? Do I keep silencing my heartache? Who was I to talk to?

For an exceptionally long time I didn't know how to process his death. I avoided thinking about his death or facing it at all costs. I thought one day I would wake up and mysteriously have all the right answers to solve the pain I'd been living for so long. Relocating from a small town to the fourth largest city in the world to attend college was quite challenging. It was a culture shock. I wasn't used to the magnitude of all the things in the city, like places to go and all the freeways. In Lufkin, everything was within ten minutes. In my new location, it would take over thirty minutes to get places. I packed up three times attempting to move back home during the first semester. But the best thing that could have ever happened to me is that I moved away from the constant reminders of hate.

While attending TSU, I received a notice about the upcoming Dean's List ceremony. This assembly appeared to be a little different than the previous ones. I was given a direct order by the University's Provost to attend, when, normally, attendance was optional. I was in my junior year and had made the honor roll each semester, but I had never received a direct order to attend. Walking in, I spoke to several classmates when someone tapped me on the shoulder, guiding me to the front row. As I was sitting there, I heard my name called.

At a university with over ten thousand students, it was common to have shared the same name as someone else. So, I sat there for a few seconds until I heard it again, "Jamie A. Byrd." *"Okay, that has to be me,"* I thought. As I peeped around my shoulders, I began to stand to my feet with a crooked smile on my face, trying not to appear nervous and confused. I didn't understand why it took the President of the University, the Provost, and Assistant Provost to call me to the stage. I wasn't sure if they realized it or not, but this was way too much attention for me. This was the day I began to process my thoughts and feelings. Six years had passed, and I was going through the motions of being a college student while wearing many hats to fill my day. I never stopped to think too much of my life or how I should feel; until that day on the stage when I received a plaque for "Overcoming Life's Adversities."

Although I accepted the honor, I felt undeserving because I was not true to myself. For years, I camouflaged my pain giving the perception that I was strong. I shied away from the attention, but I later learned to embrace it as I began my healing process. I had never seen myself the way others saw me, so receiving that award made me realize it was bigger than what I was dealing with. I thought they felt sorry for me, but in fact, they saw me as strong and an overcomer. It was after that day that I started my journey of accomplishments. My definition of being accomplished didn't mean living out my dreams and goals but accepting my truth and being okay with not being okay. Never did it cross my mind that I would break my silence and use that platform and future platforms to talk about how I was feeling and share my emotions with my peers.

Reflections

- For you, what does it mean to be accomplished?

  _____
  _____
  _____
  _____
  _____

- List five things that you will do to begin fulfilling your dreams.

  _____
  _____
  _____
  _____
  _____

- Who will you ask to hold you accountable?

  _____
  _____

Relationships

Over the years, family relationships and friendships started to waver. Although I was young, I recognized how things began to drastically change within the family. We no longer planned to meet at Grandma's house like we used to. Everyone went on their own time, and our family seemed to be falling apart.

One day, while on the TSU campus, I ran into one of my cousins. Realizing things hadn't been the same between us since my dad died, I was excited to see her. I spoke. She looked at me as if I were a total stranger and kept walking. It was evident, she allowed the family issues to impact our relationship. Her walking away represented more of the family being pulled apart. I had no choice but to accept the downward spiral of our relationship. I decided to push it aside because I thought time would heal our bond, which it eventually did. I couldn't help but think though that her behavior was a slap in the face. *How are you going to ignore me when you have been afforded a full scholarship in my daddy's memory?* Clearly, she was feeling some type of way that I wasn't fully aware of. Months later, I linked up with my other cousin who also received a scholarship, and we picked up right where we left off, as always. I was still disturbed about the other cousin's disregard; but more excited to know that my relationship with the other cousin hadn't changed. My desire was for us to come to a better understanding of what family truly means and to hear my side of what I believe caused the breakdown. As the years went by, we never addressed that day on the Tiger Walk at TSU. For me, it didn't take away the love I had for my cousins, after all, we were once like The Three Musketeers.

In 2004, Sheldon Grant came back into the picture - unexpectedly. He got my number from his sister and called me. We started talking again, and because I was in college I was trying to get through school and wasn't focused on having a boyfriend; but we remained friends and would spend time together. It wasn't until 2006 that we officially began dating and became inseparable.

While I was enjoying this new relationship, my family continued to live their lives. My sister and brother became full-time motivational speakers, going all around the world to speak messages of peace. My mom never spoke out publicly about my dad's murder. She was working full-time as Circulation Supervisor at the Public Library while also keeping my sister's son and daughter as Renee traveled. Ross even travelled to Rome to speak to the Pope.

Reflections

- List five standards for yourself that you will uphold in your relationships. This includes family members, spouse, and friends.

_____
_____
_____
_____
_____
_____

- How do you get others to treat you as you deserve to be treated?

_____

_____

_____

_____

_____

Public Speaking

Being subjected to the spotlight at the age of sixteen was far beyond my control. I knew I had to face the fear of public speaking if I wanted to keep the legacy of James Byrd Jr. alive. For someone who often got butterflies when the teacher called on them to answer questions or make a presentation, the idea of public speaking turned my stomach. How was I going to go on live television or even a talk show without fainting?

Over the years, I slowly gained confidence by emulating my two siblings who retired from the military and became public speakers. I had big shoes to fill. Not only did I have to build up my confidence, but I had to face the emotional distress I'd been hiding for years. I had to tap into the years of silence that I had tucked away. This was, and still is, a true challenge for me. Some days are better than others. I knew it had to be done and I wasn't putting my responsibility off any longer. I thought to myself, "Daddy is counting on me to carry the torch," so I had to step out of self and focus on his legacy, which was to keep Jasper at the forefront of people's mind. He was a force to be reckoned with. Very straight up, you knew what you were getting with him. No one could tell him he couldn't do something, and that was the torch he wanted me to carry.

From talk shows, media outlets, small group conferences, school presentations, and even interviewing with magazine sources, I experienced it all. Once I started, it seemed never ending. I was like an energizer bunny running on low batteries. I kept telling myself to keep going and that "I am keeping his name alive." Until one day, I had a headache that, no matter what I took, wouldn't go away. I was exhausted and emotionally drained. All of it caught up with me and caused this continual massive headache. I had to slow down. I took off so fast on this lifelong journey of sharing the James Byrd Jr. story and the significance of what happened in Jasper, Texas. I didn't properly prepare myself for the physical and mental exhaustion that would come with it. Once that spark was ignited, I failed to take care of myself in the process. I wasn't resting. I was eating junk food consistently. I was only drinking one bottle of water a day. I wasn't working out. I wasn't talking to people about my feelings. I lived alone, and when I was in my apartment it would take hours for me to go to sleep because I had to calm my anxiety after speaking engagements.

It's okay to enlighten and empower others, but I had to do it on my own timing. It's mentally and emotionally draining when people are requesting to hear your story. I didn't want to turn away anyone. I wanted to spread the "Don't Hate, Educate" message to the world. There were days when I felt as if the life had been sucked out of me from the constant speaking engagements. I had to pace myself and evaluate the source and their purpose prior to accepting because some people had ulterior motives. There's nothing more annoying than sitting in an hour-long interview and the media only shows ten minutes of it and most likely leaves out the main speaking points. This happened way too often, and it caused a disconnect between what I was sharing and what the media was saying. I understand media outlets may not have the allotted time to share the entire interview; however, it's important to understand the pain a person is reliving when sharing their story.

Reflections

Consider this: To be anxious is to have anxiety about something that hasn't happened yet. Don't let it drive you into a nervous breakdown.

Grief and Greed

Feelings of loneliness

My world crumbled into a million pieces when I finally came to grips with my dad's death. It was a feeling that, to this day, I've never felt before and quite frankly don't ever want to feel again. I was totally speechless and numb for many days leading up to and after his homegoing. I wanted to run away from it all until it mysteriously faded away. As some of my childhood friendships grew closer, others unfortunately fizzled out. At the time, I didn't feel the need to understand why my relationships had suddenly changed because I was trying to process my feelings and the new life that I now had to live. Picture that! I knew it was nothing that I had done personally to cause such a change, so I kept pressing on. Pressing on by not addressing the situation, deep down inside hoping that the situation would fix itself. The ones who became closer respected my sudden isolation and understood that I was dealing with emotions that were sometimes uncontrollable. Every time I tried talking about my dad, my eyes flooded with tears. While often fighting to hold back the tears of pain, within seconds I would be fuming with anger. Angry for the pain and sorrow in my heart that I could not control. It was even more frustrating because I had always felt that I was in control of my feelings, so to be faced with such tragedy...I could not control my sudden cries.

I grew up in a loving, happy home despite the world's troubles. But this was a different type of troubling pain, one that, up to that point and still to this day, I've never experienced before. The tough part was knowing that there was nothing I could do to change it. My dad was gone, and nothing I could ever do would bring him back. I had to face reality.

For years, I had a host of rollercoaster feelings and emotions. One day I was crying my heart out and the next day I was wanting to hit something because of the anger that raged inside. Before the death of my dad, I often heard of people acting out of rage and many times the results were never good. I used to wonder, *what could possibly make a person that mad? How could a person have raging thoughts to the point of hurting someone? My elders would often say "just keep living."* Never in a million years would I imagine myself walking down that same road of anger and rage. Although the thought of retaliation crossed my mind many times, I knew I didn't have the heart to hurt anyone despite the pain I was feeling. I reminisced over the times while sitting at the kitchen table when my mother would say, "No matter how people treat you, you don't take matters into your own hands because God will deal with them."

I grew up being quite active in church. There weren't many Sundays I would miss singing in the choir at Goodwill

Missionary Baptist Church. I felt as if I knew right from wrong, according to God's Word. But as a teenager, still growing in faith, I sometimes struggled with patience; and my lack of patience caused me to waiver in my faith. I became discouraged. My mother was not only a nurturer, but she also made sure my siblings and I stayed grounded. Once that foundation was laid, I might have gone astray, but I never forgot and would always find myself thinking about God's promises to His children. I knew, according to His word, "The Lord himself goes before you and will be with you; he will never leave you nor forsake you. Do not be afraid; do not be discouraged." Those words spoke into my spirit on many nights. Nights when I was miles away from home, laying in my dormitory bed holding back the tears and sudden outcries until I fell asleep.

For years, people used to call me anti-social because I had no problem being alone. I figured, *If I'm alone, that's less I have to worry about.* I no longer had to hide my emotions. If I felt like crying, no one would know. If I wanted to scream, no one would know. But deep down I was avoiding social groups because I was protecting my feelings. I was escaping the talk, the many questions that people had longed to ask. Who would have imagined something as simple as introducing myself would become a dreaded task, one I wanted to avoid? Many times, I held my breath after stating my first and last name, hoping no one would connect the two. Because the Byrd name was not a common name, many times people would instantly pick it up. I could see the curiosity on their face wondering if they should ask and some would say without a doubt, "Are you related to the Byrd that was killed?" With a lump in my throat,

I would respond, "Yes." I almost never acknowledged myself as his daughter until further into the conversation because I knew the questions were coming. Growing up my mom would often say, "your name defines who you are, and you should be proud of your name." I had to reflect on her words of wisdom to get me to the other side of my funk. How could I channel the anxiety and avoidance into something meaningful and powerful? Once I took control of that conversation, I felt at ease. There is something significantly impactful about controlling your own narrative. Something that sounds so simple freed me from drowning in mental distress. I couldn't let anyone take my story and feelings and use me as a pawn by talking to me; so, I limited my conversations and how much I let people know upfront and became vigilant about not allowing them to ask me certain questions.

One Saturday afternoon, my friend Kristen and her mother came to our home - unannounced. When they arrived, I was in my room (as usual) with the door closed. I heard them ask my mother if I could visit with them for a couple of hours. This was one time I was hoping my mom would say no. But of course, my mom thought it would be a great idea for me to get out of the house. Kristen was one of those friends that became distant. My mother had no idea that we were no longer close friends. I played it off well. I sat in the backseat of her mom's shiny red car and before we could drive off good, her mom looked at both of us and said, "y'all need to talk." Boy did she put us on the spot. I wasn't sure what Kristen's mom knew or was thinking, so I kept quiet. Kristen and I never discussed what was the sword in our once sisterly relationship, although things were never the same, we seemingly patched things up and remained friends. I often wondered if there was more I could have done to keep our relationship as strong as it once was. But as much as I wondered, I realized that we simply grew apart. I was forced to shift my thoughts, behaviors, and mindset due to tragedy. Whereas before I was living the life of a typical teenager, typical was no longer present for me. Many times, when I had to prepare for an interview or a trip to appear on a talk show, my friends would be planning to hang out at Jones Park. Jones Park was a very popular park in the black community. While I did thoroughly enjoy my teenage years, what I didn't enjoy was the unwanted attention and notoriety of being the youngest daughter of a hate crime victim.

Grief is a natural, human, unpredictable, and unavoidable reaction to a loss. No matter how hard you try to avoid it, you will have to face your grief. Through my trials I've also learned that grief identifies the significance of how important the relationship was. Not only was I grieving the loss of my dad and the way he died, but I was also grieving the unsatisfactory punishment granted to one of the suspects (life with possibility of parole in 2038), the dysfunctional family drama, loss of friendships, and just a week prior to my dads' death, my family buried my uncle (my mom's brother). Uncle Oscar died while on vacation with his lady friend. It was a sudden death and total shock to my family. No time to grieve. There was no autopsy. I was unable to properly process my uncle's death. It was unexpected and many questions were left unanswered. The image of my dad sitting on the back row at my uncle's wake with his dark shades on trying to hide his pain is sketched in my memory. My dad looked to my uncle as a brother. For years I became numb to it all, it just became too much to process. Burying two of my loved ones, weeks apart, was incomprehensible.

    I didn't want anyone to ask me how I was doing. Overflowing tears. Suppressed feelings. Unexpressed hurt, betrayal, disappointment. Hiding my feelings of anger and other emotions may have hindered me from accepting love from others who wanted to express their concern for me. Focused on protecting my sanity, I hoped others would abandon the conversation. Quite honestly, I would do it all over again - guard my feelings to protect myself. Some people may wonder what good comes from suppressing your feelings or even being angry? Doesn't that cause more stress? For me, it kept my expectations of people at a minimum because not everyone could handle my story. I have learned through this life cycle that people will see a sign of weakness and use it to their advantage. I've had co-workers try to exploit me to boost their professional status. I've been unexpectedly brought into their speaking engagements because of who I am. I've been caught off guard by being introduced as the daughter of James Byrd Jr. rather than by my name. People will use your story to build their platform. To this day, I still suppress my feelings to protect myself from people who only seek to benefit from my story.

Walking through the pain

It's okay to not be okay. But it's not okay to stay that way. Black people are the proudest and most unflinching humans and feel weak if they cry. It's okay to cry. Once I started to journal my feelings of pain, family greed, and friends' betrayal, I started to feel a sense of relief. I had to understand that not all people grieve the same or at the same time. For me it wasn't until I began the process of writing this book that I started to grieve and carve out all the years of unattended feelings. Twenty-three years of feelings of disappointment, resentment, embarrassment, shame, and emptiness plagued my heart for years.

We went from this reputable family to a family with members who felt entitled, and that entitlement led to acts of greed and selfishness. The tragic death of my dad left a pit of emptiness in my heart. Imagine being 39 years old holding onto so much pain while trying to keep it all together as a wife, mother, a loving daughter, friend, public servant, mentor, and many other important roles.

There are several things that help me combat grieving the loss of my dad. First, I acknowledge the pain. I no longer tuck away my pain hoping that it will magically disappear. I face the un-faceable at that given moment. Secondly, I recognize triggers that may increase my anxiety or jeopardize my mental health. I then understand that everyone would not grieve the same as me and in the same manner. I became a part of the change instead of waiting for the change. Lastly, I take time in self-care by going for a run, planning a girls' trip or even a spa day followed by some retail therapy. All these things are important to understanding and coping with the loss of a loved one. Simply doing what makes you happy, with no regrets.

Family Dynamics

Everyone in my family dealt differently with the grief of losing my father. One day I decided to sit down with one of my aunts to discuss the issues that had unimaginably struck our once positive and well-known family. She didn't give me much insight but shared her feelings of disappointment as the family went their separate ways and grieved separately rather than as a unit. I never would have imagined my family not getting together playing board games, cards, dominoes, singing, while my grandmother played the piano and cooked up a lot of food. This separation was not just between my siblings and I and my dad's siblings, although we were the first of the bunch to break away. There was division amongst his seven siblings. This was shocking to many who grew up amongst my family knowing how close we all were. After many years of being distant and handling our pain on our own, the family found its way back together. This is something I've prayed for.

Grief and Greed

When my grandmother gained her heavenly wings in 2010, I figured this would bring everyone together again, but it took a turn for the worse. My aunts formed their cliques amongst each other, while my uncle remained neutral. This caused me so much anguish. *How could a family become so divided and over what?* This was a never-ending thought that ran through my mind. I never found out what happened between the "sisters," but I could only imagine it being about positioning in the family, who took on responsibility and dominant roles. At least that's the only conclusion they left me to perceive. Entitlement comes in many different forms. A person may think because they are the oldest sibling that they call the shots or should be the first to know. In every family there is a "go to person;" that person may feel entitled to handle everything without including others' opinions because quite frankly that's what they've been allowed to do many years before, so why should things change? Then, you have that go-along-to-get-along person who always gets looked over but really wants to be included and acknowledged. We all have that Mr. or Mrs. "Always Right," and sad to say, but it happens often, family fall outs could be over monetary and material gain. These are all types of entitlements that cause confusion within families. There were so many moving pieces when it came to ours. I believe it was a combination of things that drove the separation. Their grief led to greed. Sometimes people process grief through their obtaining of monetary and material things not realizing the pain they are causing to themselves and others. I believe it is all unintentional acts. I am humbly grateful that my family is once again the loving, caring, and supportive family that we are known to be.

Hand-me-down Opportunities

My siblings and I did not feel acknowledged when it came to opportunities of sharing my dad's life and death with the world and how it affected us as his children. We desired to tell our story. Neither myself nor my siblings lived in Jasper, and it was impossible in the moment to know everything that was taking place. We trusted and depended on family to keep us involved and aware, but I'm disheartened to say it didn't always go as planned.

Too often, information was filtered down to one of us as a notice but only if it wasn't intriguing or convenient for others to partake. Some may ask why his children weren't getting the information firsthand. Due to such a high-profile crime and putting Jasper on the map, people's automatic reaction was to contact family in Jasper thinking "the children of James Byrd Jr" lived there. This went on for years until we decided to let people know how to contact us. Our main goal was not to exploit the family in any negative way, but to stay true to our feelings by letting sources know that we always had been available and open to speak, even if it was challenging.

This book was not written to disparage anyone's character. This is my story and my truth, and this is what my family, and sadly, countless others have endured. My family is at a much better place, but there's still more work to be done, and I pray for total restoration of my family dynamic and the Byrd family name.

Reflections

- What are some ways you process your grief?

_____
_____
_____
_____
_____
_____
_____
_____
_____
_____
_____
_____
_____
_____

- A family that prays together stays together.
- Pain is Not Permanent: "And we know that all things work together for good…" (Romans 8:28 KJV).

The Process of Forgiving While Remembering

Everyone was speaking about peace. I didn't want to hear about peace or forgiveness at the age of sixteen. Immediately following my dad's death, my sister Renee didn't hesitate in taking the Martin Luther King approach. She was only 27 years old. With boots on the ground, she didn't waste much time speaking out and promoting peace and love for all humankind. Juggling the role of a wife and mother of a 1-year-old little girl left her with little to no time for herself. Renee would return from one trip, and, in less than forty-eight hours, she would be boarding another flight to continue being the voice of peace and unity that the world needed at that time.

While I accompanied Renee to several speaking events, let me tell you, my approach was much different than hers. As she so proudly carried out the words of Martin Luther King, "Hate cannot drive out hate; only love can do that," I wasn't turning the other cheek. I took on the Malcolm X mentality. "Be peaceful, be courteous, obey the law, respect everyone;

but if someone puts his hands on you, send him to the cemetery." I wanted those three disgusting demons to get the same treatment they had given my dad that night. Two out of three were granted the easy way out - the death penalty with death by lethal injection- and one was sentenced to life in prison with the possibility of parole in 2038. Disappointed in and resentful of the criminal justice system for partially granting justice. If the crime was equally agreed upon and shared, they all should have received the same penalty.

To know that two of them were able to die peacefully by going to sleep is disturbing. Before he died, one of the murderers ordered thousands of dollars of food as his last meal. Because of him, there is now a cap on how much a prisoner can order prior to execution. He was also the first white person in Texas history to be sentenced to death due to killing a black man. This is where the justice system failed the Byrd family. Is there true justice, though? Since it won't bring my dad back, does justice even really exist?

Trying to process how the justice system works as a kid was overwhelmingly stressful. I couldn't understand for the life of me how one got a lesser sentence when they all played a part in killing a black man that summer night. The death penalty is a quick way to be put out of one's misery. When a person commits such a heinous crime and they are granted life in prison, if that person has any remorse life in prison would insanely run its course. There was no forgiveness left in my heart for them. Although I was against the death penalty as it seemed to be the quick fix, I also didn't want them to have the possibility of parole. Life in prison under solitary confinement with no possibility of parole would suffice as far as I was concerned.

One Saturday, nearly six years after the Jasper lynching, while cooking and cleaning with the television chattering in the background, I heard the words, "dragged behind a pick-up truck." I was caught off guard. My hands started shaking. I slowly walked toward the television and heard the reporter recounting an incident that was a reenactment or a copycat killing of my father's murder. A noose hanging from a pick-up truck. The word NIGGER written across the truck. I wasn't paying attention to the television initially, but those words arrested me. Those words jolted all my triggers. Who could be so cruel? Who would think it was okay to imitate something that shocked the world? I was rattled to learn that this incident happened not too far from where I was living at the time. I was unnerved. Lost my appetite. Couldn't sleep. I was discombobulated the rest of the day. I lived alone at the time and all these thoughts flooded me. Will someone come after me? What do I need to watch out for? *I live in a big city. This shouldn't be happening here. Doesn't this only happen in small, down-South country towns?* Wrecked is the best word to describe what that news story did to me. I mentally prepared myself not just for news channels to start calling for interviews and reaction, but for reports after reports weighing in on the copy-cat killer. Nothing surprised me anymore. Shockingly, though, the media never contacted me or my family about that incident. We got the chance to deal with it privately rather than publicly.

If I heard anything that triggered me during that time and over the years, I would sit with it until I could find some peace. In that peace I removed the bothersome aspects of the trigger. I took the power over the words by not reading too much into the stories being shared. I knew the media would say anything to increase viewership, so things would be spun out of control. I took the situation at face-value instead of allowing the words to take control of me. I prayed, often asking God to help me through the pain. I prayed the Lord's Prayer daily. I asked God to protect me, comfort me, and remove the fear of the unknown. Once I covered myself in prayer, I felt as if I was able to handle anything that might come.

After the copy-cat incident, I tried to find a new way of life by working and bringing normalcy to my life without my dad's murder always being at the forefront. I built a new identity by serving others who had gone through crisis. I did it at work. At church. Schools. I worked in low-income communities and tried to show them they could get out of their current circumstance – if they chose to. I wanted to be an example of someone who made it through a very tough situation, so my message has always been that we must learn how to make the best of the hand we are dealt. We must ask ourselves how our story can help others in their situation.

By the beginning of 2012, I told Sheldon we had been together for too long to just be dating. I told him there were others waiting to snatch me up, which was true, but I didn't want them. I wanted him. By 2013, he proposed. I said YES!!! We quickly started the wedding planning and paid for the venue that same week. We got married July 25, 2014, and I transitioned from a patrol officer to a community service officer by October of the same year.

We immediately started trying to conceive, but it wasn't until 2016 that we conceived our son. The summer of 2017, I was writing in my journal about the joys of finally becoming a mother. God came to me as I was laying in the bed looking at the ceiling, searching for more words to describe my soon-to-be-born son. When He said "forgive." That wasn't the word I was looking for. So, I kept staring at the ceiling and again He said, "forgive." Tears streamed down my face and could not be restrained. "Oh, this is surely not what God wants me to write about my baby." That's what I told myself about what I heard. I continued to write words of affirmation over my child, but forgiveness never left my mind. Finally, I put my pen down and said, "Okay God, what is it that you want me to do?" Although I knew exactly why He placed that word in my spirit, I wanted confirmation because a part of me didn't want to obey God. Within seconds, my face was covered in tears and my shirt was soaked. I then surrendered and asked God to guide me through something that I vowed to never do - forgive those murderers. As I was talking to God, trying to find the most appropriate names to call them instead of demons, nothing came to mind. I said, "God knows my heart, He knows my next thought before I think of it, so why am I trying to trick God into thinking I feel one way but really feel another?" He then spoke the word "curse." When I heard that word, I realized that the curse would be the unhappiness I could pass on to my child. I didn't want my child's spirit to absorb the negative thoughts that I had about the killers. I knew that if I didn't truly forgive them for my own peace of mind, I would knowingly transfer this curse on to my child. I knew that if I did not forgive and break the curse, the unforgiveness would forever be in my spirit and control a part of my life that I didn't want it to control. I began to cry out and praise Him like never before. I was being delivered from the negative thoughts and pain I had wished upon my father's killers.

Over two decades later I no longer carried those same resentful feelings as teenaged Jamie did. Through growth and maturity, I learned to channel my anger into fuel for change. At that time in my life, it was imperative that I sought forgiveness within my heart for me to grow, prosper, and be aligned with God's divine purpose for me. This was not easy at all. I kept telling myself that I had every reason not to forgive them and God would understand why I had straddled the fence for so long. Many of us are the sum of our experiences. Life happens, and those experiences will either make you take a step back and reevaluate your life or continue to live in a downward spiral. The question I often ask myself is, "How can I empower?" Overcoming oppression for me as an African American means to never say never. I had always promised myself that I would never forgive them for what they did to my dad and my family. But as I matured and experienced different walks of life and people, I learned that forgiveness is not for the other person, it's for self. As I started my journey to forgiveness, I began to purge those hidden feelings and hateful thoughts that kept me in bondage for so long. I needed to be restored mentally and spiritually. Not only did I need a renewed heart, mind, and soul, I needed to be freed from all sinful thoughts and spoken words.

While I still have vivid thoughts of the numerous places in which my dad's body parts were strewn on that dark, gloomy summer day, I can still walk this forgiveness path with grace. Remember, no matter what you go through, you can overcome, you can thrive, you can get through to the other side. I got to the other side through having devotion time with the Lord, meditation, and recognizing my truth, despite others' opinions of me.

Fullness and Completion

After experiencing the type of tragedy that the Byrd family did, it can be difficult coming to a place of fullness and completion in your soul. The trauma alone can zap you of even the desire to feel. I spoke regrettable words to my dad hours before he was killed. Once those words left my lips, I was never able to take them back. Unbeknownst to me at the time, those would be my last words to my father. I decided to write him a letter asking him to forgive that 16-year-old Jamie. I asked for forgiveness because I needed peace to help me continue through life. I no longer wanted to isolate myself or those feelings of disappointment. I wanted to stay connected to God's promise, which is peace and prosperity; and, for me to be feel worthy of his many promises upon my life, I wanted to release those hurtful words, "I Hate You" from my lips and cast them in the pit of fire. I will no longer feel guilty for something that was not of me but of evil.

I went through a forgiveness exercise to help free me from the unforgiveness that had gripped me. I forgave the part of me that had unforgiveness for myself. I forgave the part of me that made a covenant with evil to protect myself from others hurting me. I forgave that part of me that was wounded and held on to the pain and the trauma of the situation between me and my dad. I came out of agreement with every negative curse I knew the enemy tried to place over my life because of my dad's murder.

I sought the Lord and asked Him to cover me with His blood and integrate my soul to a place of wholeness and completion in Him. Then, I repented. I repented for screaming at my dad and telling him, "I hate you!" I know he was only trying to spend time with his family. I also had to repent for stating publicly that I wanted those "three demons to be dragged behind a pick-up truck to their death just like they killed my dad." Those words were so violent, and I could not live with myself knowing I had said that about them.

Finally, I had to forgive my dad for not giving his family one hundred percent of him when we needed his support. I forgave him for what he may have thought was good enough when to me it really wasn't. I forgave family members who were deceitful towards me and my siblings. I forgave the family members involved in withholding information and opportunities that were intended for me and my siblings.

The whole process of forgiving myself, repenting, and forgiving my dad was like a cleansing for my soul. I got something I didn't even know I was missing; I began to feel joy deep within. I did all of this while still remembering the place he held in my heart and trusting that God could fully fill the void left from my father's murder.

Remembering His Name

More than two decades later and James Byrd Jr. still didn't get the honor he deserves. Due to the spike in racial injustice, several cities are unveiling "Say Their Names" Memorials. These names exhibit Black Americans whose lives have been lost due to social injustice, police brutality, and racism. It was disheartening to know that many have forgotten about James Byrd Jr., the black man who was slain in Jasper, Texas. It saddens me that the Statewide James Byrd Jr. Hate Crimes Act as well as the Federal James Byrd Jr. and Matthew Shepard Hate Crimes Prevention Act have been forgotten by many. Is it because it was over a decade ago? Is it because justice was served and now, we can overlook the hateful crime committed by three white supremacists? I hope he is not just remembered as part of a hate crime statistical data but as a father of three who fought like hell to go home to his family. What must we do to remember the evil, tragic death of a black man in Jasper Texas on June 7, 1998? Let's start by educating our young adults about the James Byrd Jr. State and Federal Hate Crimes Prevention Act. SAY HIS NAME, "JAMES BYRD JR."

Besides fighting to get these bills passed, I personally sit on the board of the Anti-Defamation League (ADL), which is a national organization that fights to stop defamation and secure justice and fair treatment for all people. I also sit on the social action committee of my sorority, Delta Sigma Theta Sorority, Inc. to ensure everyone has the right to vote and receive fair treatment. I truly believe that as a community of people, we must ensure that these moments of hate become movements toward peace and equality.

Reflections

- God is going to reveal some stuff to you during your process of forgiving. As you begin to forgive, write down what the Lord is saying to you.

It's A Movement Not A Moment

From the day my dad was killed, I had several choices to make. My choices were to either hate those that killed my dad, hate the entire white race, act out as a teenager, or take a profoundly egregious situation and turn it positive. Although I was taught to love all humankind, my heart held so much hatred toward those three individuals. This was something I definitely had to pray about, which didn't come easy. Hating the entire White race was not fair because the White race didn't kill my dad. Acting out as a teenager would have brought more pain upon my family. So, I had to make a choice, and I chose to be the change that I wanted to see in others by promoting love. I began to share my story with anyone who was interested. Boy, what a drastic change that was for me!

I mentioned earlier in the story, that all my life I had been a shy but outgoing person that hated to be called on by the teachers. Back then, I wasn't in a place of peace and forgiveness, and I was just going through the motions. But, by the time

I had my son in 2017 and went on this journey of forgiveness, it forced me to come out of my shell of timidness. I quickly started to make special appearances in front of hundreds of individuals in school auditoriums speaking on panels and being interviewed by news media and talk show hosts. I had taken "being the change I wanted to see" to another level. Public speaking was never, and still isn't, something I love to do, but it's something I must do to keep my dad's name alive. Sometimes we must get uncomfortable to create needed impact not just for us but others. Over the years, I have become less uncomfortable with telling my story and sitting through an hour or longer interview while fighting to hold back the tears. Now, I must be spiritually led to share my testimony while making sure all my emotions are intact. Some people wonder why I'm a little hesitant at times when speaking out, and I tell them, "Everybody shouldn't get front row seats in my life, and not everyone is worthy of hearing my testimony. There's a time and place for all things."

Throughout my experiences, I've learned to decipher when to accept and when not to accept speaking opportunities. You know, not all invitations are meant to be accepted. In the beginning, I was always available even if I had to rearrange my schedule. I would not have missed telling the world about my dad's tragic and fateful night. If I had to decline for certain reasons, I would think about it days after with feelings of disappointment and guilt. This went on for many years until I realized the mental, emotional, and physical effect it was having on my livelihood. That's when I learned to be okay with saying, "Thank you for the opportunity, however; I will have to decline at this time." Saying this for the first time felt as if a ton of bricks was lifted off my shoulders. But I could do that by this point because I was in a place of forgiveness and knew more about protecting my emotional peace. My point to you is, yes, tell your story because if you don't someone else will. But do recognize the good sources and bad sources and pay attention to signs of distress you may feel when being asked to share your story. Move at your pace, according to your own purpose and no one else's.

Reflections

- Process Pain and turn it into Purpose

> Bible Verse: "Yet what we suffer now is nothing compared to the glory he will reveal to us later" (Romans 8:18 NLT).

Becoming a Change Agent

How can I empower others to be change agents? You must find something that is important to you and fight for it. Erasing hate was important to me so I became a part of the solution and not the problem. I joined the police academy to protect and serve the communities in which I live and work. I'm an active board member in organizations - like the ADL- where I also sit on the Women's Initiative committee, and I participate in lobbying for legislation related to equality, fairness, and justice for all people.

I get so much fulfillment as law enforcement when I get a message from a teen or young adult telling me they appreciate me for talking and listening to them. I meet kids where they are, and this allows them to identify with me. Through me they can see overcoming is possible, and we've been able to bond over our stories. They trust me with their story because I shared mine with them. They have gone off to college and still check in on me and my family. They let me know they are praying for me. I've been used to help change these kids' lives, in a time when police officers are not favored in some communities.

Through the Women's Initiative, we speak on numerous platforms to women who've faced discrimination in the workplace, domestic violence, and other types of discriminatory issues. We work to legislate for and pass more bills on women's rights. By these women being a part of this type of initiative, it gives them resources to help them manage through their situation and see their circumstances change for the better.

The Afro-American Police Officer's League, where I serve as the Grievance Director, went to lobby the State Capitol for the George Floyd Justice in Policing Act. My father's death even made him a change agent because his vicious murder caused the State of Texas to execute the first white man for murdering a black person.

My siblings continue in their professions as full-time motivational speakers and lobbyists with the State Hate Crimes Bill. Ross did activism work with the late Dick Gregory,

Martin Luther King III, and Mamie Till, the mother of Emmitt Till, who was violently murdered by white men for allegedly whistling at a white woman. Two of my aunts were present at the White House when the Federal Hate Crimes bill was signed into legislation in 2009 by President Barack Obama.

Many have asked how I did it. How did I manage to keep focused and complete all the things I aspired to accomplish while all along being reminded of the tragedy that knocked on my door the summer of 1998? I replied, "I made a plan and a promise to myself that I would not be defeated by life's circumstances, nor would I allow those circumstances to determine my future." My purpose was to talk to young people because of the age I was when I experienced the greatest trauma of my life. So, it was God's plan for me to reach that age group to help pull them out of their tragedies and help them see how they could triumph over them. At their age, they are still moldable, and I knew that if I could get to them early, they wouldn't have to face years of processing their pain like I did.

I no longer wanted to waste time staying in that dark place where hibernation had set in for so long. It was always my intention to go to college, graduate with an undergraduate and graduate degree, start a fulfilling career, get married and have a child. All those things were desires that I was able to accomplish. I then decided to move-on-purpose by overcoming my fears. The fear of public speaking, the fear to speak MY truth, the fear to be bold within myself and accept the things that are unchangeable. Moving within my purpose didn't mean everything I dreamed of would magically appear. For me, it was the opposite. Nothing happened overnight. I had to realign my mindset and position myself around new people to help me mentally and emotionally accomplish my dreams. I've never had any professional counseling, but I was encouraged by the new people I surrounded myself with, like deans and professors at TSU that treated me like a daughter. Supervisors I worked for took a liking to me and held me by the hand. I could no longer wallow in my own pity, and they gave me something to strive for. My older sorority sisters guided me through life. I leaned on a lot of them to get me through. They would invite me to Sunday dinner and welcome me into their families. That was my way of coping with my situation. Sometimes when a person moves within their purpose it may take them experiencing many failures before reaching that goal or that successful moment. Matter of fact, I had several pitfalls, but I savored the experience of each obstacle because I knew the result was bigger than me.

I could have been disgruntled. I could have played the victim at every life challenge that came along the way. But I knew the choices I made would have ultimately defined me. No matter what you go through you have the power and choice to overcome and thrive to your highest potential. Keep believing and trusting in God and He will change your life for the better according to His will.

Joining the Force

The history of policing began with slave catchers and protecting the interests of the slave owners. During that time, it was popular for officers to have the hunter-prey mentality. Some seem to think not much has changed. In the beginning, I struggled with the decision of joining the police force due to the perception and history of policing. I decided to join the police department to be a beacon of light to others who have lost loved ones due to a heinous crime and to combat racism. When people hear the word "police," they automatically think someone is going to jail. Prior to joining law enforcement, I've had more positive than negative experiences with the police. Although I do understand that's not the case for most black people, especially black males, my goal is to change the face of policing. The more officers begin to look like the communities in which they serve, the more comfortable black people will be around them.

Making arrests is only one component of law enforcement; it is not the core of policing. Serving the community in the capacity of bridging the gap between the police and the community is the foundation of the department. The community holds the key to policing and if officers don't engage and get the input of the citizens, we will never bridge that gap. We will continue to have the "us against them mentality."

While working in a predominately black community I want to restore the safety and trust that has been long broken. My goal is to restore years of distrust that began with the police abusing their authority while wearing the badge. This is just not a white versus black issue. Officers of all ethnicities and backgrounds are guilty of acting unnecessarily above the law. In current times, we must recognize issues from all aspects; it's not just about being afraid of white racist cops because whether we want to admit it or not, all cops have the potential to become corrupt by the power of the badge, IF they embody a weak mind and misled spirit.

It's much more common to hear of a white cop violating the rights of a black person or even killing a black person than it is a black police officer violating or killing a black person. This is because the criminal justice system has failed black people for many years by not holding white people accountable and sentencing them to the proper punishment. The question is, why is this so? Is it because they feel as if they are more superior? Is it because they are convinced the criminal justice system will find them innocent as history has many times proven? Let's not remain in a place of despair, but let's do our part as individual citizens by calling out the bad cops.

Wearing the Badge

I took an oath to serve and protect all people while enforcing the law of the land. From the day I applied, I envisioned myself spreading knowledge, guiding people, and building trust within the community. I chose to work in a predominately black community to help rebuild years of broken relationships between the community and the police. Throughout my tenure, I've seen good policing and bad policing. I made a promise to myself while taking the oath that I will never take a backseat to shedding light to unjust situations no matter the race, ethnicity, or gender.

The police department is a big place. Either you fit in, or you don't. While in the police academy, it was clear I was not a "go along to get along" type of person. There was a cadet who said he was going to "put a vibrator up" an intimate part of me. I got in his face and told him he needed the job more than I did and that he didn't get to talk to me like that. I thought I handled it by confronting him. The following week I was pulled out of class and questioned about the incident. Come to find out another cadet casually mentioned it to a sergeant at church that Sunday. This sergeant worked at the Academy. He identified the wrong in the situation, sexual harassment, and reported it that Monday. I shared what happened and assured my supervisors that it was handled. They responded, "That's good, but now we are going to handle it." I was still new and not yet aware of the investigation process. Three months later, he was fired. Several in the class thought I was the one who told on him, but I didn't. Some cadets spread rumors about me and told people to watch me because I would get folks fired.. Almost two years after becoming an officer, I had to hear those rumors until the person who actually reported him was revealed. The female officer who casually mentioned the incident to a Sargeant (not realizing the magnitude of the incident and how policy frowns upon these type of incidents) later apologized for unintentionally putting me in the spotlight. Whether reporting him to get him in trouble was intentional or unintentional, I didn't hold it against her. I never told anyone, and she was grateful to me for not exposing her. I did let her know, though, that she cared more about the cadets' friendship than I did, and it didn't matter to me what they thought of me.

They became self-aware of their actions. I've had my car keyed, and two tires flattened while at work. Notes would be on my car saying, "I see you." When I reported the notes to a sergeant, I was told, "Maybe it's someone who likes you." This sergeant was not my regular supervisor, so he showed no interest. After reporting the vandalism to my Lieutenant, W. Kennedy, and Sergeant J. Meyers, they were infuriated. Attempting to catch whoever was doing this, they disallowed my personal contact information from being available, even to other officers. They also instructed me to park in a secured parking space where security cameras were visible. Doing the right thing, even when no one is looking, was not a common practice for some.

Police officers see the worst side of humanity. I will never forget being a rookie and reporting to a call at a convenience store. Upon my arrival there stood a young boy, around the age of thirteen, with no shirt on, bleeding profusely from his back. During the investigation he explained that his mom beat him with a wrought iron because he stayed late after school to play football when he was told to come home to keep his younger siblings. I began to get emotional on the inside while trying to outwardly appear strong. I began to pray to God for strength as the welts on his back triggered images of my ancestors being beaten. I knew this was just the beginning to a career full of gut-wrenching images.

Over the years, I've been on the scenes of children being victims of rape and abuse, countless homicide victims, the bloody mangled bodies of human trafficking victims, battered victims of domestic violence, suicide by cop, meaning civilians who pose as a threat, have something deadly in their hands, which would provoke the officer to ignite deadly force to eliminate the threat in order to protect innocent bystanders, and much more. As a first responder, we wear many hats. We are called to protect and serve, nurture, counsel, educate, encourage, and inspire. I've had many experiences of walking the halls, sitting at the lunch tables, and entering the classrooms of students that only see police officers when someone is taken to jail. I want little black kids to know that it's okay to be and trust a police officer despite what they see on TV, social media, or even what their families may think. How can we make a difference if we are not given the opportunity or properly guided and given the tools and resources to be the change? I vowed to do my part and change the image of policing in the black and brown communities, but I am also adamant that we need to stop hurting and killing people in general.

For me, everything is not about black and white. When we look at the statistics of crime, black-on-black crime is higher than any other crime. We kill each other in our own neighborhoods. A life is a life regardless of the color of the person whose life is being taken. We can march and chant all day that Black Lives Matter, which is true. But when will we recognize that ALL LIVES MATTER! When are we going to get fed up with all the symbolisms and fancy chants and demand solutions? I'm all for letting our voices ring in the streets as we march, but WHAT'S NEXT? When will we take a stand? Ask yourself, are you really tired of seeing headlines of black people dying simply because of the color of our skin? When will our skin color no longer be a crime? Then ask yourself, "How can I get involved in my community?" I understand the frustration and energy leading to protests, riots, and marches, but again, WHAT'S NEXT?! We must fortify our own community to no longer become victims of racism. Enough is Enough! The Movement must prevail! No Justice, No Peace!

Make a Difference and Make It Count!

Travesty and Injustice

It's more than just individual officers and it's more than municipalities, there's a history of systematic racism that's deeply rooted in the justice system. Politicians may say officers need more training on de-escalation, use of force, ethics, culture diversity, and many other classes to help guide officers when situations occur. I believe continuing education by providing more training is always a plus. We must get rid of the language of racism within the criminal justice system before attempting to train officers to treat black people fair and equal.

Too many officers are policing communities they can't relate to, and some are overly nervous and allow their training to be overpowered by fear. I'm often asked, "Do you get nervous when dealing with an irate or aggressive citizen?" My answer is always, "Yes, depending on the situation." An officer once told me, "The day you become complacent and not nervous of certain situations, it's time to find another profession." At the time, I didn't understand his point. But later in my career I realized that it is perfectly normal to be uneasy entering certain situations, but it's not good to let complacency take away the human aspect of fear resulting in someone getting unjustifiably killed.

Over the years, there have been countless murders by the hands of white nationalist cops. A black female found dead in a jail cell after an altercation with a cop. Traffic stops resulting in fathers being murdered in front of their children. Black churches being riddled with bullets and burned. A black man sitting in his apartment shot and killed by a white police officer. Police officers using excessive force by having a knee on a black man's neck for nine minutes and twenty-nine seconds (9:29) silently killing him in broad day light. A black female shot and killed by police officers as she lay in the comfort of her bed. A young black man hunted down and shot while jogging in his neighborhood. A black man being accused of assaulting a white female in a park. All these acts were egregious and, unfortunately, the list continues. Open wounds are hard to heal when there are constant pickings at the scab.

I am a mother of a little black boy who will one day grow up to be a successful young man. I dread the day I will have to sit my son down and tell him not all cops are heroes despite how he views Mommy in uniform. I dread telling him that he will most likely grow up being judged and treated differently due to the color of his skin. I dread telling him that he may face adversities and discrimination despite his qualifications solely because he is a black boy in America's society. How do we fix this problem that has plagued the black community for centuries? It's not for the black community to fix. There's something wrong with the way racism has shaped the images of this country. White society created racism; therefore, it's not the responsibility of black people to teach about racism. Think about it, we can eradicate racism in this country if we genuinely want to, but ultimately, it's about the funding and the politics of the game and whites remaining the majority.

Once we realize that racism was produced by race and we are all members of the same race, which is the human race, we will be a better country. But until then, we are not free, nor are we equal.

Reflections

- Once racism is completely eradicated from the criminal justice system then we can have a fair and equal justice system.

Finding Peace Within the Pain

Losing a loved one can be a very traumatic time in one's life. There were times when more than one emotion seemed to take hold of me; now that was scary. For years I was running on empty while my mind was going a thousand miles a minute. I didn't allow myself to internalize the death of my father nor did I open myself up for anyone to help me through my pain. I figured why be a bother when many people were dealing with their own wars of life. So, I thought, "What good will they offer me?" I also was afraid of rejection and people being judgmental of my feelings and thoughts, so I kept it all balled inside. My inner self was screaming for help, but I was too private to open up to anyone. Somehow, I had to find peace within my pain.

In the years since my father's death, I've never sought professional counseling. Strange? Maybe. I didn't see how it could help me. Sit on a couch. Tell a stranger my story. They pull out their book, which holds no real answers to help me unlock the pain. I think not! On the outside I didn't look like what I was going through, so I chose not to talk about it, even to those who were in my circle of trust. It's too sad to talk about even to those I love dearly, like my siblings. It hurts to talk about it, so I don't want people to see me in such an emotional state. I don't want pity. I needed another way.

The way came in the form of my sorority sisters who would call me at the right time, a time when I was sad and lonely. One called me on a Saturday, at eight o'clock in the morning, asking if I wanted to go to breakfast. We laughed and hung out. That lifted my spirits. Changed the way my day could have gone. My college deans and professors would get me out the house to grab a bite to eat. I'm not sure any of these people realized how much their phone call pulled me through some tough days. Reflecting on the various ways I found peace in the pain, speaking engagements, and sharing my story, on my own terms, was therapeutic. If you've faced something tragic, so heinous that it brings pain thinking about it, don't talk about it until you are ready. Don't let others manipulate you into telling your story!

I started a tradition of creating an annual vision board. Planning out how I wanted my life to be. I encourage you to get a poster board and create your vision. Visions aren't supposed to be hateful, negative, or filled with the disappointments of your life. They're filled with courageous thoughts, fearless dreams, and intentional plans for your life.

Surround yourself with positive people who are going to encourage and not judge you. I have that in my husband, Momma, siblings, sorority sisters, and a handful of people

I connect with. My husband and son help me maintain my peace. Sheldon makes my life easier so I can focus on whatever I need to get done. He is so supportive and a true partner. I don't have to say anything, and he knows what I'm feeling. My son notices little things about me and acknowledges them, like if I get my nails or makeup done, he will say, "Mommy, you look so pretty." That warms my heart. Connect with the people that warm your heart when you're in their presence.

Working out, especially running, brings me peace. Sheldon decked out our whole garage to ensure I have a safe place to exercise and relax. Find your "safe place." It doesn't have to be a physical place like inside your home. It can be a safe place in your mind, body, or soul. It could be reading a book you enjoy, meditating, playing old board games with friends. Find things that bring you joy not just happiness.

Retail therapy helps me relax. It temporarily takes me out of the negative feelings and gives me something else to focus on. I also get to buy things I either want or need. If shopping isn't something you enjoy, go to the park or a nice restaurant and people watch. That's fun all by itself. I also have a standing monthly appointment to get a massage and facial as a part of taking care of myself. When walking through a healing journey, like I have been, it's important to practice self-care.

How else did I find peace while living through the pain? I asked God to remove the hatred from my heart. I asked God to cleanse my heart from all malice and ill thoughts towards those three demons. I had to learn to separate the demonic spirits in them from the people they were so that I could go through my healing journey.

There are many ways a person may find peace while experiencing pain. For me, it was the deliverance, being true to myself and my feelings, despite anyone else's opinion. Understanding my position now is not dictated by my position of the past. Marching to my own beat and not allowing anyone to exploit or take advantage of me, for political accomplishments, and to forgive and let go.

Things happened in life that I couldn't foresee, but God never took His hands off me. I refused to let the heaviness weigh me down and force me to miss the promises God has for me. My internal scars are fuel to my faith. The scars don't mean that I am finished with the race, the scars mean that I am healing - by His stripes - and I must continue to move by faith and not by sight. I thank God for restoring my mind and my heart. Although I felt as if the odds were against me, I kept praying to God for His grace and mercy to bring me through the tragedy and the oppressions of life.

When I look at my emotional scars, I don't want to think of the pain I went through. I think of the Grace of God. Something has to die in order for something to be birthed (John 12:24). The literary birth of my book, *Triumph Over Tragedy*, and the passing of my paternal grandfather was the divine fulfilling of the scripture.

I no longer have to live with despair and unforgiveness. As I reminisce over what my life was and what it could have been if I didn't make a change in my heart, I think about Sam Cooke's famous song, "A Change is Gonna Come." A change had to come for me to live with peace and prosperity. I am a living victory.

Missing You

What a journey it has been to fight through this profound change in my life. Although my father and mother had long divorced, they had put aside their marital differences and remained cordial towards one another. Matter of fact, the day before he was killed, they were chatting and laughing like old lovers. Nothing was perfect in our household, but it was perfect for us. Neither parent showed interest in getting remarried after they divorced, and I often wondered why. Probably because my dad was too much of a social butterfly for anyone to take him serious enough for a relationship. My mom had always been such a nurturer to her kids that she would often say, "Girl, I don't have that kind of time," she would always follow that statement with, "plus, I'm set in my ways."

So many of my good memories were overshadowed by grief. As a little girl, it was almost intimidating being around my dad. He was so tall and thin. He wasn't very playful with me and my siblings, but when there was an audience, he was energetic, playing basketball with the kids in the family.

He was the fun uncle to his nieces and nephews. He was so protective and strict that I went to my mom for everything because she was more willing to say yes. When he came to Lufkin to visit us, it was often a surprise. He would walk in like he lived there. One time he popped over, and I said, "How you just gonna pop up over here?" My mom laughed, but he saw it as me talking back. My mom knew I was playing with him. He didn't.

So much of my grief was based on the relationship I didn't get to have with him. My sister, Renee, had a stronger bond with him because she was already a teenager in high school by the time my parents got divorced. I spent most of my time with him during the three weeks of some summers when we visited Jasper. While I didn't have a typical daddy/daughter relationship with my father, I still loved him and knew him as my daddy. There was no doubt of who he was to me because our mom wanted to ensure we still had our own personal relationship with him regardless of whether they were together or not.

At my graduation ceremonies, my wedding, and the birth of my son, I wanted him there to say, "my baby girl." I wasn't mentally prepared to not have him be there on the day of my wedding. I wanted him to walk me down the aisle to give me away to Sheldon as a sign of his approval of Sheldon and our marriage. The months leading up to the wedding were extremely difficult. I couldn't fathom the thought of his absence, but I had to get through it. I had his picture pinned on my bouquet, so as I walked down the aisle, he was right there with me cheering me on as my brother so proudly escorted me, leaving the honor of cheering me on to my mom as she was smiling with great pride. Boy, that was one of the hardest things to endure during the ceremony - him not physically being there. I made a promise to my brother that I would not mess up my make up going down the aisle. From the moment my brother held my arm, he began to crack jokes. He had me cheesing from ear to ear and before I realized it, I was at the altar. This helped ease my mind and kept me focused on being cute and not messing up my makeup. Once I made it through the ceremony, I needed to keep myself together during the slide show I had put together of those special moments with my dad. One of the pictures was from our last family reunion where my brother and I were on each side of him. There was a picture of him holding me as a baby, and other random pictures of him by himself. There was another picture of him playing the piano. I don't believe there was a dry eye in the building. My heart smiled knowing that he was proud and cheering me on.

    He wasn't very affectionate; however, he had a way of showing you he cared. He would always put his hand on the top of my head, which would drive me crazy because I didn't want my hair messed up. But he would pull my head close to him to reassure me he was there and that he was proud of me. Once I became a police officer, I knew if my dad were alive, he would have shouted from a bullhorn, "My baby girl is a law woman." He would have used that to his advantage and tell everyone I would put them in jail if they did anything to him. I'm laughing as I write this because it's almost like I can hear his voice saying those things.

Two years after getting married, my husband and I were expecting a little boy. Oh, what I would have done to have my dad be a part of our new bundle of joy's life. I could hear him saying, "Lil ol' girl, what you doing having a baby?" While he did get to experience being a grandfather to Renee's oldest child, who was one year old at the time, he never got to experience me, his little girl, having a child. Many close friends and family would tell others how protective he was over me and my big sister. My dad didn't like for us to wear shorts above our knees and shirts with our arms out. No matter how old we were, he always saw us as his little girls. So, to see his reaction to me having a baby would have been quite interesting. I have plenty of stories and videos to share with my son. He will know the life and death of his "Pawpaw," and I pray my dad's legacy is carried on through his grandchildren.

What I learned from that unnecessary disagreement with my dad, the day before he was murdered, is to never say things that you really don't mean. Remember to always say I love you, no matter what. You never know if it will be your last time with that person. You don't want the last words they hear from you to be words of negativity and anger.

We should always remember that the tongue holds a lot of power, so we should be careful of what we say and how we say things to others. The Bible tells us, and I will end with these two scriptures:

Ephesians 4:29 (TPT) says, "And never let ugly or hateful words come from your mouth, but instead let your words become beautiful gifts that encourage others; do this by speaking words of grace to help them."

James 1:19-20 (NIV) says, "Everyone should be quick to listen, slow to speak and slow to become angry, because human anger does not produce the righteousness that God desires."

Dear Daddy,

There are so many occasions I wish you could have been a part of, but I know you are in a better place, looking down on us and protecting us from the evils of this world. I often think of you and wonder what you would think of all your kids, grandkids, and great grandson who carries the middle name James. I do know one thing, you would be bragging to everyone, like you often did. All these things that you couldn't be present for, not of your own fault, cause me to reflect and realize that I miss you still to this day. This is a journey that I am still walking through and there will always be a void in my heart from when you were murdered. I realized now that parents are assigned to us for a specific amount of time and the only one that is to fill that gaping hole of their passing is the Lord. I reflect on the good times and not so much of how you died, Daddy. You lived an honorable life, James Byrd Jr. Although you are no longer here in the flesh, you are with me in spirit. My true Guardian Angel! I miss you so much.

Your baby girl

Reference

1. Casas, A. and Bailey, C. (2021, June 2). *Race in America: The legacy of the murder of James Byrd Jr.* Retrieved from https://www.bbc.com/news/av/world-us-canada-57285785

Memories

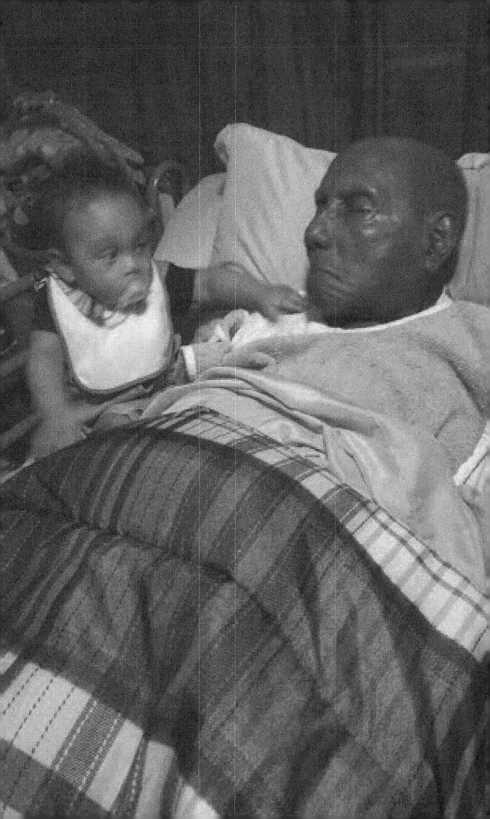

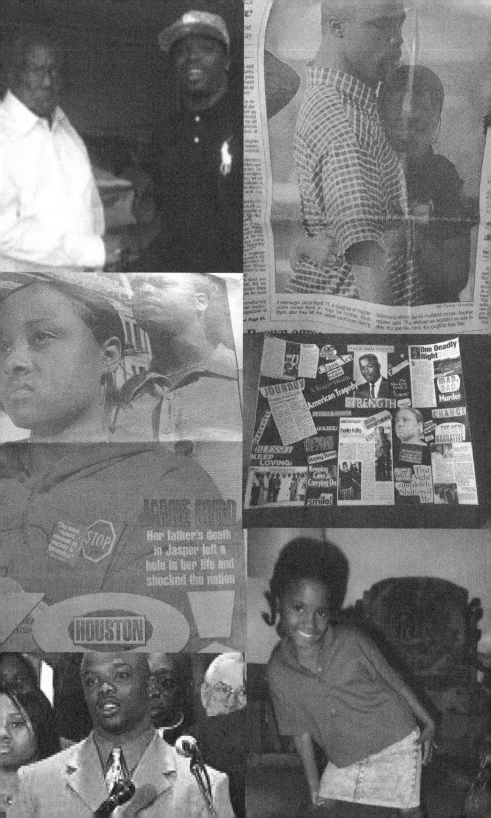

Made in United States
Orlando, FL
16 August 2022